# THE DEAL

ISBN: 978-0-9913542-8-3

Library of Congress Control Number: 2020916038

# THE DEAL

## Chuck Neff

MATER
MEDIA

*For my lovely wife, Judy. Thanks be to God for permitting me to walk into your life.*

*And for married couples everywhere. The world needs you to be a great couple, a lifelong witness to the love, mercy, and forgiveness of God.*

**1**

My name is Charlie. And I am a jerk. If you talk to the people who know me best, and if they're honest, that's a word they might be throwing around. They still remember the time I missed a wedding anniversary to play golf in California. That same weekend I also missed my daughter's birthday. Come on, she was only two.

How could anyone expect me to pass up a round at Pebble Beach along the spectacular 17-mile drive near Carmel-by-the-Sea? A good friend asked me to play with him and two potential West Coast clients on one of the world's most beautiful and celebrated courses. How could I say "no" to that?

Why do some people obsess over celebrating an anniversary on the exact day of the anniversary? We went out for a nice dinner a few days after I got back home. So, what's the big deal? And my daughter's second birthday? Wasn't I there for the first one? And unless we told her, a two-year-old wasn't going to remember if I was there or not. If that's being a jerk, then maybe they're right. But that golfing weekend turned out to be the beginning of some professional relationships that have now become the foundation of the biggest deal of my life.

"Excuse me, Sir!" A slight tap on my shoulder pulls me out of my wistful daydream. "We are about to take off. Would you like something to drink?"

"Sure! How about some red wine?"

This is my flight from San Francisco back home to Denver. This return trip has consequences far bigger than just me. The bank accounts of people in two law firms are about to be fattened immeasurably.

I had been in the City by the Bay for a few days as part of some final talks on a merger between my law firm and another group in nearby Palo Alto. The talks would be the final step in putting together a deal that would provide a sound footing for growth and financial stability for everyone in both organizations. As the lead negotiator, I had been promised a lucrative bonus if I could make it work. This deal would change everything for everyone. I'm guessing right now no one in my law firm in Denver and no one on the West Coast might be thinking I'm a jerk.

Honestly, I think I'm a good person. Sure, I have some bad days. At times I tend to get angry, frustrated, and upset when things don't go my way. I'm a bit impatient when red lights seem to be red too long. I have been known to yell at televisions when referees make so many obvious bad calls, especially the ones that go against my beloved Broncos. And don't try to cut in front of me in rush hour traffic! That makes my blood pressure skyrocket. So, I'm not perfect, but I think most people can easily see I really am a decent kind of guy.

My colleagues would say I am a pretty good lawyer. Successful, for sure. A partner in the law firm. A father with two kids, Robbie and Julie. A husband who has been married for a good number of years to my wife, Nora. If I'm honest about it, she is a remarkable lady. Good mother. Big heart. A perky smile. Sparkling brown eyes.

She has a habit of biting her lower lip when she is lost in some deep thought. Our life together has been pretty good. A bigger-than-I-ever-imagined income. An attractive all-brick, two-story, four-bedroom house in a good neighborhood. Two cars. One for Nora and one for me, although I'm a bit embarrassed to say mine is a vintage Porsche 911 SC. Essentially we have pretty much anything we want and would ever like to have. Not bad for a small-town kid who grew up in western Nebraska.

This flight should be a time of celebration. Heading home to pop champagne, giving high-fives and pats on the back to my partners and colleagues. But my mood right now feels more like a flat diet soda than the red wine I'm sipping. I'm having trouble wrapping my mind around the reality of how unhappy I am. The misery is stifling. The sadness is dark. It feels like I'm shrouded in a heavy, wet blanket squeezing the air out of my chest. This deal should be cause for great jubilation. It is anything but that.

Nora is the center of my attention. And it is not a "good" attention! All of her endearing qualities don't seem quite so endearing right now. The truth is they are downright annoying. A grim, bleak gloominess in our marriage is taking off the luster of what should be a magical time. Things aren't so good between us right now. In fact, they are horrible. I don't think the kids know anything is wrong. But our tempers are short. Disagreements run rampant. Yelling at one another seems to be commonplace.

This marriage is nothing like I thought it would be. I have given her virtually everything she has ever wanted. The money, the clothes, a beautiful home. Everything! It's the so-called American Dream. But the chasm between us seems to be bigger and mightier than the Colorado River thundering through the Grand Canyon. I don't get it.

What happened to us? Where is that young couple who was so madly in love, ready to take on the world, so confident about the road in front of them? We were so full of love and laughter. Life was an adventure and it was fun. Walking in a park and relishing a picnic lunch of bacon, lettuce, and tomato sandwiches with a can of cold pork 'n beans was more tantalizing and memorable than all of those expensive steak dinners, bottles of Cabernet, and cherries jubilee at the Brown Palace. What happened to the life we imagined? Where did those simple times go when the two of us were all that mattered? Were our dreams a sham? Did we not see that the world would get in the way and turn us into a sad and unhappy married couple?

Life right now is as bleak as anything I have ever experienced. The loneliness is suffocating. We live in the same house, but we might as well be living miles apart. When the two of us head off to bed at night, we end up lying with our backs to one another, not speaking. Good-night kisses are all but nonexistent. Most nights I am unable to fall asleep. Tears often fill my eyes. Some nights I can hear her sobbing quietly. But I don't ask her about it. Part of me doesn't care.

The irony of this flight back to Denver is it's the same flight I took back home from Basic Training right after we were married. That time I couldn't wait to get home and be with my new bride. We had been married only a few months when I was sent to Fort Ord, California. That four months away from each other seemed like an eternity. We couldn't wait to see each other again and get on with our life. That flight so many years ago had me crammed in a middle seat in the back of the plane. That flight seemed like we were traveling in slow motion and seemed to take forever to get me back home to my sweet wife.

At the time we lived in a small, one-bedroom apartment near the campus of Denver University. We drove a used, beat-up Volkswagen with a bad paint job. We were a young, starry-eyed couple with great hopes for a wonderful life together. The truth is that back then we had nothing. The odd contradiction is that we seemed to have everything.

I should be madly and crazy in love with her. But I am not. I don't feel anything for her. In fact, I'm not even sure I know what love is anymore. Today feels so different.

As I sit in a cushy leather seat in first class, I realize that this flight is moving all too quickly and forcing me to deal with a situation I honestly don't want to face. My cute wife doesn't seem so cute these days. I suspect she doesn't think I'm too cute either. The two of us live our lives like strangers, wandering around under the same roof without much in common anymore. We seem to be going frantically in different directions, doing different things that have little to do with each other. I have my life. Nora has her life. What happened to "us?" When did our life together as a couple begin to fade away and vanish?

The questions keep ricocheting around my mind. What happened to that couple that was once so full of life, ready to tackle the world and make our dreams real? I remember how we looked forward to building our life together and sharing the adventure in front of us. We just knew we would be a couple unlike so many others, laughing and loving each other deeply and passionately all the days of our life.

All of that now feels like a make-believe fantasy. It all somehow seems phony. Maybe we were just two naïve kids pretending to be "big people," like the times my older sisters and I rollicked around our grandparents' attic playing dress-up in their old clothes. We probably thought we knew everything and had all of the answers to life's biggest questions. How silly! Now I am one of the "big people" and this life is nothing like I imagined.

All of those hopes and dreams of our life together are now a distant memory. Those plans have effectively been crushed. Did we really believe our life together could be different than all of those other seemingly stale marriages we were seeing everywhere? I think we thought so. But now it seems as if we are just like all of those married couples we didn't want to be like. The world tells me that we have everything.

The truth is it feels like we have nothing.

"Ladies and gentlemen, this is your captain from the flight deck. We are beginning our descent into Denver. We expect to be on the ground and at the gate in about twenty-five minutes."

The nearly three-hour flight has raced by. Now I have a decision to make. I need some time to sort this out. The biggest deal of my career is less than a week away from being finalized. Clouding everything is this marriage of mine, which has become a nightmare threatening to destroy the only life I have ever known. A foreboding ache has turned my stomach into a battleground of emotions. The anger, fear, disgust, and shock have me feeling utterly confused. I don't think I can go home to Nora. Not right now. The most disturbing part of everything is that I need to figure out a way to tell her it's over.

# 2

My turmoil-filled mind was so full of random thoughts, I hardly remember retrieving my luggage or getting to my car in the airport parking lot. Interstate 70 looms in front of me. The highway will take me west. A few miles ahead Interstate 25 will head south toward home. As I approach the interchange and the exit ramps, I find myself inching over into the far righthand lane to begin a dubious northerly trek that will take me who-knows-where.

Going home doesn't seem to be a good option. I need to catch my breath. A little stretch of time away from the tumult and chaos of a family I know will be waiting for me. I simply am not ready to walk back into a world I know doesn't like me very much right now.

I'm scared. The knot in my stomach is making me feel like I want to throw up. The road might as well be a dark alley, narrow and threatening, with its shadows reaching out from the walls like sinister monsters ready to swallow me whole. The fear is growing.

I haven't been this frightened since the day our little Robbie needed open heart surgery. Shortly after his birth, doctors discovered a tumor that had stretched his tiny heart to nearly three times its normal size. He would need surgery to fix it.

As Robbie was wheeled down the long corridor to the operating room, Nora and I clutched our hands tightly. It seemed as if we were holding on for dear life, all the time praying the little guy would make it through what would be several hours of a tricky and delicate surgery. As he was being wheeled out of his hospital room, he moved his head back and forth from one side of the gurney to the other stretching his neck to catch one more glimpse of his mom and dad. I am sure he had no idea what was going on as this pack of strangers in blue hospital gowns towered over him and escorted him down the long hallway.

The odds were good the surgery would be successful. But we didn't know. Would this group of doctors and nurses do what they told us they could do? Would Robbie be okay? Would our son have to suffer? What would the rest of his life be like? A barrage of questions for which we had no immediate answers.

The doctors spent nearly six hours repairing Robbie's little heart. Everything turned out just as everyone had hoped it would. We were relieved beyond words. Our hopes had been realized. Our prayers had been answered.

But that was then. This is now. And this marriage seems beyond repair. No one can fix this. No one can mend these two hearts of ours that have now grown cold and hard. I have this overwhelming sense that things are out of control and traveling at something close to the speed of light. I find myself gasping for air and my fingers are beginning to tremble. Life as I know it is about to change forever.

I know I need to call Nora to tell her I won't be coming home. I had been rehearsing what I would say for a few days. But even now I have no idea what words to use. Maybe there aren't really any words to use when your life is about to explode into a thousand tiny fragments. Life as you know it with all of the good times and the not-so-good times is going to be splattered against a wall of bittersweet memories. Maybe it's only natural that words fail in a time like this.

Wherever this drive ends up taking me, I need gas in the car. One of our long-established stops along Interstate 25 north of Denver is Johnson's Corner, a 1950-ish truck stop, known everywhere for its amazing, scrumptious cinnamon rolls. We would always plan our camping trips into the mountains west of Fort Collins to include enough time to stop there. Camping trips weren't camping trips without a stop at Johnson's Corner. That exit is now less than an hour away. My plan is to stop there, fill up the tank, and make the knotty phone call home.

The sun is beginning its gentle, rhythmic dive behind the rolling foothills and mountain peaks to the west. The sunset will no doubt be one of those spectacular fire-in-the-sky moments with all of its reds, oranges, pinks, and purples splashed against the evening's baby blue sky and white, wispy clouds.

The interstate traffic is moderately light for a Thursday evening in the middle of May. The humming of the car engine and the road noise combined with a long day of travel are lulling me into a slight daze.

The distant sound of a siren diverts my eyes to the rearview mirror. Flashing red lights on what has to be a state highway patrol car are getting bigger. As I slow down and edge to the right shoulder to make sure the patrol car has enough room to pass, the cruiser pulls in directly behind me.

You've got to be kidding. What in the world could he want with me? A slight twinge of anger and frustration begins to well up.

The trooper eventually gets out of his car and makes his way toward me. Rolling down the window, I'm doing my best to sound cordial and unaffected by whatever is going on.

"Yes, Sir! What's the problem?"

"License and vehicle registration, please."

"Sure, but what's the problem?"

As I grab my wallet, fish out my driver's license, and fumble for the registration in the glove compartment, I ask again, "What's the problem?"

The trooper monotones, "Speeding! Seventy-four in a 55-mile-per-hour zone."

"The speed limit along the interstate is 70 and I was only going 74? Come on, Officer! You've got to be kidding me!"

Taking my license and registration, he says, "It's a construction zone. Fifty-five is the speed limit."

"A construction zone! Really?"

Now I am starting to get angry.

"There was no one working there. Either they weren't working today or they went home. And I certainly wasn't the only one going that fast."

"No, you weren't the only one going that fast. But you are the only one I pulled over. And the speed limit is still 55."

My temper has now ignited like a Bunsen burner in a chemistry lab. I say it again, "You've got to be kidding me. Don't you have anything better to do?"

He looks up from the papers with a slight shake of his head. "Your lucky day, Sir! Like winning the lottery!"

Thinking my legal connections around here might make a difference, I blurt out, "Do you know who I am?"

The trooper sighs and shakes his head. "Yes, actually I do know who you are. You are a smart-alecky speeder driving your flashy, little sports car who was going 19 miles an hour over the speed limit in a construction zone. And a mouthy and arrogant one at that, I might add."

The fumes of fury are rising in my throat. Keeping my mouth shut is a challenge. I could have one of my law clerks fix this thing in a matter of minutes with a phone call to the county prosecutor. Our firm tries cases in this area all the time. In fact, I probably know his boss.

"Look, Mister…" He glances down at my license. "…Landis!"

"That's right…Landis. Charles Patrick Landis. Height – six-feet-one. Weight – 183. Date of birth – November 24th…"

He holds up his hand and interrupts. "Mr. Landis, I am perfectly capable of reading. Stay put. I'll be right back."

As the trooper turns to walk back to his car, I yell out the window, "It was a damn construction zone. And there were no workers. Zero workers!"

With that, the officer slowly and deliberately turns around and comes back to the car. Leaning down into the window, he looks me squarely in the eye. In a calm, quiet voice, he hisses through his clenched teeth, "Mr. Landis, I would highly encourage you to check the attitude." With that he turns and heads back to his cruiser.

Tapping my fingers on the steering wheel, I sit for what seems like ten or fifteen minutes, rehashing the day, mulling over the merger deal with what are soon to be our new partners on the West Coast, and thinking about the dreaded phone call I have to make to Nora. And now a speeding ticket! You've got to be kidding me.

I finally hear the trooper's car door slam, and I see through the mirror he is slowly striding back to the car.

"Mr. Landis, your driving record is pretty good. And you were right! There were no workers and you weren't the only one going that fast. So, I am going to just give you a warning tonight."

The trooper looks at me as I sit there trying to calm down.

"Mister Landis, this is where it might be a good thing to say something like 'thank you.'"

"Thanks," I mumble irritably through my pursed lips.

He nods, hands me back the documents, and adds, "Pay attention out there. Lots of spring construction going on. Lots of workers. Have a good night."

With that, the officer heads back to his car. I start my engine, roll up the window, slowly pull forward along the shoulder, merge back into traffic, and continue the drive north.

I whisper under my breath, "What a load of crap! Like winning the lottery! My lucky day! Yeah, right! You big jerk!"

**3**

It's a busy night at Johnson's Corner. Dozens of big rigs slowly lumber around each other, trying to find a parking spot or heading back to the interstate. The hum of the diesel engines is a cacophony that rumbles and shakes the depths of your soul. The racket is constant, jarring, and at times almost alarming. The only escape from the din is inside the truck stop's restaurant.

Once inside, the memories of our time here come flooding back. The tables and roomy booths with the red leather seats where we would order our cups of coffee and those yummy, lip-smacking, legendary cinnamon rolls. They were sticky, thick, and generously wrapped in layers of sugar and cinnamon.

Nora would methodically and delicately use her knife and fork to unwrap the roll. Like a fine jeweler, she would meticulously cut off about an inch at a time, stick a fork in it, and slowly take a bite. She seemed to savor every part of the dough with all of its gooey concoction of succulent sweetness. It would take her about fifteen or twenty minutes to get to the center of the roll and finish it.

Not me! I was more like a construction worker with a hard hat demolishing and tearing out a bathroom wall. A two-fisted-let's-get-to-the-center-of-this-roll-as-quick-as-I-can sort of guy. Less than five minutes and that sweet pastry was history. I remember smiling and laughing with her about how different we were in so many areas of our life. Even when it comes to eating a cinnamon roll.

So, push those memories aside. That's all history. Make the call, Buddy Boy. Make the call!

Big breath.

I can feel my heart beginning to race and beat more rapidly as the connection is being made.

One ring.

Two.

Maybe she's not home.

Three.

She picks up in the middle of the fourth ring. "Hello." She sounds like she has been rushing to get to the phone. Her hello is as perky as ever.

"Nora. Hey, it's me, Charlie."

Her perkiness changes quickly to chilly. "Oh, hi! Where are you? I thought you'd be home by now."

I find myself searching for the right words.

"How was your trip?"

"The trip? Oh, it was good. Everything went well. The deal is in place. Contracts should be finalized and signed next week or the week after."

Silence.

"Look, Nora. I know things aren't good with us right now. I don't know what to do, but I need a little space. I need a few days to think about this. About us!"

I can hear her start to cry. Her sobs are muffled, but I know her well enough to know I have probably stabbed her in the heart. "Where…?" She can't finish the sentence and her voice is now so soft I can barely hear her.

"Where am I going to go? Well, I think I am going to head back home to Scottsbluff. I haven't called Grandma yet, but I think she'll let me hang out there for a few days."

"Why, Charlie? Why don't you come home and let's…just the two of us…talk this out?"

"I just need a day or two. Nebraska is only a few hours north. Getting there tonight will give me tomorrow and Saturday. I'll be home on Sunday."

Her words are even softer now. A mere whisper.

As I say good-bye, my heart is shattering. I want to say "I love you" before she hangs up. But I don't. Those words of endearment seem so hollow and dishonest to say at the end of our phone calls these days. The fractured pieces of my heart are exploding. The shrapnel is tearing my insides apart. None of this feels like love at all.

My walk back to the car is like some slow-motion march down a dark alley on a moonless night. The shadows of the gas pumps and the large canopy over them are gloomy and foreboding. The incessant rumble of the diesel engines drones on, but I barely hear any of that. Life right now is as muddy as anything I have ever experienced. The fear and uncertainty of the life in front of me is stifling any of the outside noise. Even the merger deal doesn't seem all that appealing anymore. At least, not right now. The only life I've ever really known with a woman I thought I could spend the rest of my life with feels like a lie. All of those hopes and promises seem to be a mirage, a dream that is flitting away into the nighttime sky of northern Colorado.

The drive north on Interstate 25 puts me into a trance, of sorts. I feel numb. Traffic is light and I set the cruise control around 65. That will hopefully get me through any construction zones without getting pulled over. The sun has dipped below the horizon. The evening sky is growing darker. The lights of Fort Collins are reflecting onto the low-hanging clouds that now blanket the sky. I know where I'm going, but I'm not in a big hurry to get there.

# 4

Fort Collins is the largest city in northern Colorado. With a small-town feel, it is nothing like Denver with its sea of surrounding suburbs. Fort Collins is the county seat of Larimer County and home to Colorado State University. The Poudre River meanders through the heart of the city.

Lots of memories for Nora and me along the Poudre. The camping trips into the Poudre Canyon. The hiking. The rafting adventures. Those amazing times now rocket back into my heart.

Just the two of us. No kids. Living life and loving each other. So simple. So magical.

Nora is an outdoor history buff. A walking encyclopedia of knowledge about the Rocky Mountains.

"Did you know, Charlie, the river's original name is Cache à la Poudre? It means 'cache of powder.'"

"Yes, I do, because you tell me every time we come up here." And we would laugh as she would say, "Well, I'm going to enlighten you again." She would go on to tell the story of the French trappers in the

1820s who were caught in a snowstorm. The only way, she would remind me, that they could preserve their gunpowder was to bury some of it along the banks of the river. Hence, the name!

For me, things on those camping trips were simple. All I wanted to know is whether the river was wet and if we had a place to pitch a tent. A little running water wouldn't hurt either.

When Robbie and Julie were old enough, we brought them along with us. Nora seemed to always find a way to teach them something about the mountains. "Did you two know the headwaters of the Poudre sit at an elevation of some 7,000 feet about a hundred miles west of here?" No, they would say, as they groaned and rolled their eyes. "Well, it does. And it flows through the Roosevelt National Forest and tumbles down the slopes of the front range into Fort Collins." The Poudre, she would add, is Colorado's only nationally designated *Wild and Scenic* river. A little mountain trivia never hurt a camping trip.

Our autumn trips were the best. October and the aspen trees. When the wind blew, the golden leaves shimmered and swayed to a score it seemed only God could have orchestrated and directed.

During the summer months the aspens were just part of the mountainside greenery. The shape of the tiny aspen leaves was distinct, but from a distance it was often difficult to distinguish the green aspens from the green of all the other trees blanketing the mountainside. But when the temperatures began to change, summer gradually relinquished its grip and autumn began to gain the upper hand. The aspens would then begin their measured transformation from green to a splendid yellow gold. Blowing in the wind, the golden leaves would burst into a glittering radiance that sparkled like the sun reflecting off an ocean. It was a dazzling display of God's majesty draped across the mountains of Colorado.

Our favorite camping site along the river was the Kelly Flats Campground less than 45 minutes west of Fort Collins. We discovered it shortly after we moved to Denver. "BK" is what we called it. Before Kids! We would spend most of the day hiking. Then late in the day we would make our way back to the campsite, where we would build a fire to warm ourselves and take away some of the chill of a long day in the forest. It was a simple time to sit around the fire and truly live the present moment. No words needed to be spoken. It was one of those times to just "be," when I think we both believed we were doing exactly what we were supposed to be doing.

October meant the higher elevations were beginning to get snow. The whiteness of the mountain peaks jumped out gloriously in the dimming light of the nighttime sky. The evening I remember most vividly is the one Nora and I knew a full moon would light up our campsite and the night before us.

We were not disappointed. As the moon rose high above the trees, it looked like a giant saucer in the sky. It was so big that I felt like I could reach out and touch it. I could see that proverbial man-in-the-moon with the greatest clarity I had ever seen before. It felt like this man up there was looking down on us like we were the only two created beings in the universe. If anyone else was out there, they didn't mean a thing.

Charlie and Nora had each other and that was really all that mattered.

I can still hear the gentle crackling of the fire. The ever-present rumble of the river roared less than thirty yards away. Our small dome tent was big enough for our double sleeping bag. It was our humble, cozy, weekend-away-from-home hangout.

For some reason that particular night, we were able to pick up a local radio station. We rolled the car windows down and danced to the music from the radio. We held each other close. With Nora's arm on my shoulder and my arm around her thin waist, we danced. And we danced…and danced…and danced. The melodies, the words, the rhythm of the music, all of it, drawing us closer and closer. The night was dreamlike.

As we sat around the fire, I looked at Nora. Gosh, she was beautiful. The glint of the flames flickering and prancing over her stunning face. Her soft cheek bones and button of a nose. Always a modest amount of makeup. A bit of eye liner surrounding her stunning brown eyes. They sparkled as she talked about everything and nothing. The sound of her voice was soft and soothing. So encouraging at times. So firm in her convictions when she stood up for what she believed was right. Her contagious smile. Her red lipstick only added to her radiance and the wonder of the night.

I remember thinking how striking and special this cute lady was on those camping trips. This night was one of those times when I found myself marveling at how truly blessed I was to be her husband.

Time had a way of standing still in those moments. Nora would sit cross-legged before the burning logs. I would lie on my side, head resting on the palm of my hand. As we looked at one another, our eyes oddly didn't seem to blink. It was like they were locked together in a deep, almost soul-searching instant. It was as if we were staring into the depths of our hearts.

Something in the moment of the night pulled and lured us closer. It seemed as if a magnet was slowly drawing the two of us toward one another. Reaching out to hold hands. The touch of her long fingers on mine. A mutual, peaceful tug would draw us even closer.

Our kisses. So gentle, affectionate, breath-taking.

The intimacy.

The closeness.

The passion.

Embracing and holding one another. Tenderly enfolded into each other's arms. That moment when we only wanted to be with one another. When truly nothing else mattered and we didn't want to be anywhere else in the world.

I remember wondering if this was what God meant when he told us that in marriage "two would become one." At moments like this, I knew exactly what he meant. I could feel it. We were living it.

Those were the days. Yes, indeed, those were the days! The operative word is "were." The reality is that those days are gone. Over.

Those times now seem to be swallowed up in the history of a couple who thought they could change the world. Those moments so many years ago have been choked into a deepening slumber of old, nearly forgotten memories. They seem to be packed away in a chained section of my heart. To be honest, part of me yearns for some of that again. In fact, I find myself wanting to smile at the memory of those days in our life. But I can't even force a smile. The truth is I'm not sure I even want to try.

# 5

The "You Are Leaving Wyoming Welcome to Nebraska" road sign means I still have about an hour before I reach Scottsbluff. A small rain shower is beginning to dampen the road. It is a slow, steady drizzle, which shouldn't slow me down too much. Fittingly, it seems to be a dreary end to a dreary day.

Scottsbluff is located in the panhandle of far western Nebraska. Along with my three older sisters, this is where I grew up. After graduating from high school, our family moved to Kansas City. My dad worked for the Union Pacific Railroad and was transferred there. My sisters were out of the house by then, but I made the move to Kansas City and from there attended Creighton University in Omaha. Since then, I have been back to Scottsbluff only a few times. The last time was four years ago for the funeral of my grandfather.

I had stopped in Cheyenne to get a cup of coffee and call my grandmother to make sure it would be okay if I spent the weekend there. I knew she wouldn't object. I also knew she would be surprised.

We haven't talked in a long time. Hearing her voice, I think she was beyond surprised. More like shocked that I was calling. And then calling so late.

"Is everything okay?"

"Yes," I lied. "I can explain things in the morning when we have more time and I'm not so tired."

"Well, sure. Yes, please come. It will be great to see you again. I will wait up."

"You don't need to do that. Just leave the door open. I can find my way inside and figure out where to crash."

Grandma cleared her throat and slowly and emphatically with her Nebraska determination and grit said again, "I…will…wait…up."

"I sort of figured you might say that. I should be there by 10:30, 11:00 at the latest. Thanks. See you in a bit."

Scottsbluff, the town, is named for Scotts Bluff, a goliath of a rocky mound that rises about 800 feet above the plains of western Nebraska. The massive bluff, which sits a short distance south of the city, was named after Hiram Scott, a clerk with the Rocky Mountain Fur Company who died near the bluff around 1828. No one knows if he was sick with something like cholera or maybe had suffered a serious injury, but for whatever reason, Scott was unable to continue the journey. His party surprisingly left him behind. His remains would be found near the bluff. From that point on, the landmark became known as Scotts Bluff.

For some four decades in the 1800s Scotts Bluff served as a landmark to help guide several hundred thousand brave pioneers along the Oregon Trail. To the Plains Indians, like the Pawnee and Sioux who lived in western Nebraska, the bluff was known as "me-a-pa-te," which means "the hill that is hard to go around." Vestiges of the trail still dot the landscape, a vivid reminder of the ferocious courage of those trailblazing legions of daring men, women, and children who left everything they ever knew and headed west to the promise of a new and hopefully better life.

Growing up in the city of Scottsbluff, I don't think I really appreciated the history of the trail. Maybe it's like someone growing up in a place like Washington, D.C. So much remarkable history is rooted there. From the men and women who made the tough decisions to help shape our nation to the monuments and museums that remind everyone of what it took to build a country unlike any other in the world, that city contains a collection of incredible, amazing, and notable stories of so many extraordinary and striking moments in time. All of that history is there, but I wonder if the people who live there might take all of it for granted. I know, for me, the history of the Oregon Trail was a piece of history that simply happened to be part of the city where I grew up. I knew a bit about it, but it really didn't seem to be a big deal.

Then as a freshman in high school I made the cross-country team. Our long runs would take us off the school campus, south for several miles through the communities of Terrytown and Gering, and then west along a road called Old Oregon Trail, which today is a two-lane highway. If you look closely, grassy swales running parallel to the pavement mark the path of the original trail. Running those many miles day after day, I began to realize the significance of what really happened along this narrow strip of ground.

From 1840 until about 1880, as many as 400,000 people used this trail to head west. From the trailhead in Independence, Missouri and all the way to the lush green valleys of Oregon, the entire overland adventure covered 2,170 miles, which could take as many as five to six months to cross. Navigating their way by Scotts Bluff meant the pioneers had completed only about a third of the undertaking. This enormous stone bluff also served as a harbinger that the Great Plains were behind them and the rugged Rocky Mountains were next.

On a good day the wagon trains could cross about fifteen miles of the flat prairieland. A hard-driving wagon master could sometimes forge out twenty. The rigorous journey was hot, dusty, and dangerous. Historical accounts indicate that five to ten percent of the pioneers died along the way. Most of the deaths were attributed to diseases like Asiatic cholera, which became known as the "unseen destroyer." Accidents also accounted for a large number of deaths.

Running long distances provides a lot of time to think and be by yourself. The routine can often be boring and monotonous. The time can also turn into a personal encounter with all of God's creation. The Oregon Trail was no exception. Turning westward, the old trail would begin a gentle uphill climb toward the bluff. The rhythmic sound of my breathing and running shoes hitting the ground would take me back to those bygone days more than a century ago.

I would begin to imagine those vast numbers of pioneers heading west, steering dozens of prairie schooners toward the steep stone cliff of Scotts Bluff towering along the north side of the trail. On the south side is what is called the South Bluff. It is not as large, but it is big. The gap between the two mammoth landmarks is known as Mitchell Pass, named after Brigadier General Robert Mitchell who helped establish a small Army outpost during the Civil War to protect not only the western territories but also the growing throng of pioneers heading to Oregon or the ones who had had enough and decided to settle in the area.

Because of the incessant, howling winds, Mitchell Pass before the Civil War was known as the Devil's Gap. Running through the Pass on most days meant a head-on battle against those whistling gales. With head down and pushing into and through the stiff winds, I would race back in time to imagine the dust of the slow, plodding wagons heading west. They kicked up a heavy cloud of blowing dust that seemed like a dense bank of fog. As I ran on, trying to catch up with what I visualized as the back end of the wagon train, I could almost begin to hear the sounds of the wagons lurching and slogging over the prairie.

The booming voice of the wagon master leading this entourage through the grasslands.

The loud, relentless chatter of the men driving the livestock.

The hollering of other men and boys leading the oxen and horses pulling the wagons.

The women walking next to the wagons were yelling to keep their children close by and away from the massive oxen and horses staggering under the heavy loads packed into each wagon. Riding in the wagons was so rough, it was easier to walk. Only very small children, the sick who could not walk, and the elderly who could not keep up the steady, day-long pace were confined to the wooden carriages.

It was difficult to imagine what their emotional experience must have been like.

The fear. Borderline panic where the only option seemed to be to keep going.

The courage. A daring attitude to embrace the unknown and stay the course.

The perseverance. A tenacity to overcome the daily setbacks and not complain about them.

The determination to build a new life in a place they had never seen.

A tenacious pioneer spirit to believe in what could be and then find a way to do it.

My headlights zoom by a mile marker, which slaps me back to the reality of this dark, rainy night. The sign tells me Scottsbluff is only seven miles away. My grandmother lives on the west side of the city. So, I am pulling into her driveway before I know it. As I turn down the gravel road leading to the old farmhouse, the lights from the car flash through the drizzle to reveal a weather-beaten sign that has been there since I was a small child.

## WELCOME TO THE HOME OF
## BEN AND MARY LANDIS

The driveway snakes its way through a grove of trees for about a hundred yards. As I listen to the echoes of the tires on the wet, crunchy gravel, I can see the porch lights go on. My grandmother, all five-feet-four-inches of this stalwart, one-time schoolteacher, walks out in a blue robe and waits under the large overhang. The farmhouse is a white, two-story frame home. When my grandparents sold their cattle ranch, they kept the house and about an acre of land.

Dashing through the light rain, I quickly run up the three steps to the landing. Our embrace is warm, like all the hundreds of times we've hugged one another in the past. Her long gray hair is pulled back in a bun. Her blue eyes, peering through her wire-framed glasses, are kind and inviting.

"Charlie, it is so good to see you."

"Me, too, Grandma. Thanks for letting me come up. And apologies again for the late arrival."

As she takes both of my hands in hers, she looks directly into my eyes and says, "I'm so glad you came. But this isn't good, is it?"

My chin drops. My eyes look away. "No, Grandma, it's not good."

"What's happening?"

"It's Nora. We aren't doing so well. Everything just seems to be falling apart."

With that, she throws her arms around my waist, pulls herself close, and buries her head in my chest.

"Charlie, Charlie, Charlie!" Her voice is soft and choked with emotion. "I am so sorry. What can I do?"

"I don't know."

Then trying to deflect the emotion and pain of the moment, I say,

"Maybe let me come inside and show me where I can get some sleep! Let you get some sleep, too! I'm guessing you are up way past your bedtime."

We both muster slight smiles, and with my arm around her shoulder, we head inside.

I am tired. We can talk more in the morning as I begin to sort out what this life in front of me is all about.

**6**

Blazing through the open window, the morning sun startles me out of a deeper-than-I-expected sleep. It takes me a second to turn my head away and focus on the nightstand's alarm clock. The red digital numbers glimmer 5:29. Sunrise in western Nebraska comes early this time of year.

Throwing back the covers and climbing out of bed, I am not hearing any other activity in the house. Grandma must still be sleeping. But walking out of the bedroom toward the kitchen, I see her sitting in the living room. A candle is lit beside her chair and an open Bible covers the corner of the coffee table next to her.

"Grandma," I whisper as if someone else were in the house sleeping. "What are you doing up so early?"

"Praying! It's what I do every morning about this time. It seems I need to be storming the heavens with a little more fervor and boldness today."

Yeah, I think to myself. Not that anyone or anything can fix any of what is going on, but maybe prayer is the only way to set things right.

We both sit there for another minute before she pushes herself up and out of her chair, heads to the kitchen, refills her coffee mug, and pours a cup for me.

Coming back into the room and sitting down, Grandma asks the question for which I'm not going to have a good answer.

"What happened to the two of you?"

"I'm not sure really. You know, work is good. The firm is growing. A mega-deal on the West Coast is taking a lot my time. Traveling, meetings in Denver and California, lots of phone calls, working weekends and nights, pulling all of the details of this merger together. I'm quite excited about it. This should be good for everyone. More money, prestige, a plan to really put us on a nationwide legal map, so to speak."

Grandma is listening. I can tell she doesn't seem impressed.

"That's great, Charlie. But what happened to the two of you?"

"I don't know, Grandma. I really don't know. It's just not the same. Our marriage is nothing like I expected."

"So, what did you expect?"

I don't have an answer. Only a casual smirk and a shoulder shrug.

Grandma is not saying anything either. She looks at me waiting for an answer. I still don't have one.

"You know, I pray for the two of you every day. Actually all of the children and grandchildren, but lately you and Nora have been on my mind a lot. Almost to the point that it seemed God was telling me to pray especially hard for you. Like something wasn't exactly right with the two of you and the kids."

I don't really want to talk about this. I don't understand how this sweet, spry grandmother living so far away could possibly know anything might be wrong with us. Praying for us? God telling her something might be wrong with us? I don't think so.

I'm agitated and uncomfortable with wherever this conversation is going. It's taking everything inside of me to be considerate. I've got to. She's my grandmother.

"What do you mean you pray for us every day?"

With that, Grandma looks to her Bible on the table, reaches over, takes some piece of paper out of the back, and holds it up in front of me.

"What's that?"

"It's your wedding invitation. When I started praying more intensely for you, I searched the attic and fished it out of our family album. I save everything, you know."

As she smiled, she handed it to me. A bit yellowed and frayed around the edges, for sure. Wow, I didn't think anyone saved this stuff.

> *Mr. and Mrs. James Edmond Sullivan*
> *request the honor of your presence*
> *at the marriage of their daughter*
> *Nora Ann*
>
> *to*
>
> *Mr. Charles Patrick Landis*
> *on Saturday, the eleventh of June*
> *at twelve o'clock Nuptial Mass*
> *Saint John the Baptist Catholic Church*
> *Marshfield, Wisconsin*

As I read and re-read the invitation, Grandma finally asks me, "What do you hope happens while you're here?"

"I'm not sure. Get some space. Take some time to figure this out."

"Well, when we sold the ranch, Ben took some of the money and built a small log cabin out back. I'll leave it open for you. It might be a little dusty, but I've left it just the way it was before Ben died. Maybe it can be a bit of a sanctuary. A place to get away. It'll be quiet. No distractions. No television. No radio. A small library of books. Some religious statues and a few crucifixes on the wall. It's where Ben would pray and spend time in what he called 'the silence of time to check out reality.' I used to kid him a lot that everything he put out there made it look more like a shrine than a log cabin."

I remember seeing the cabin when we came back for Grandpa's funeral four years ago. But things were so busy then, none of us ever went inside. I can tell by her smile and the way her eyes light up that just talking about her gentle Ben, as she liked to call him, is bringing back a lot of fond memories of their life together.

"Thanks. Maybe some quiet time there will help."

Ever the honest, straightforward grandmother, she pauses and asks, "So, have you thought about talking to a priest?"

That's exactly the question I do not want to hear from her.

"I don't think a priest is going to help this."

"But we've got a terrific priest here in Scottsbluff."

"I don't care how 'terrific' he is. I really don't want to see a priest."

"But you know him."

"What? How would I know him?"

"You went to school with him. Fr. Bill Donahue."

"Billy Donahue! Wild Bill Donahue! You're kidding. He's a priest? Grandma, I can't believe that!"

Billy Donahue was a year ahead of me in school. We were altar boys together in elementary school at St. Agnes, our home parish. Then in high school we played varsity baseball on the school team and in a summer traveling league. He was a great hitter and a good outfielder with a strong arm. He went to college on a baseball scholarship. Billy was a crazy man, a live-in-the-moment buddy who didn't seem to care a whit about classes or grades. Or about God!

We became good friends over those years. He was one of the most popular students in school. Tall, good looking, and very athletic. We didn't go to parties together, but we did hang out a little after school

32

and on a weekend now and then. If you could believe what a lot of people were saying, Billy Donahue was wild and unruly.

That rowdy personality worked its way onto the baseball field, too. He played hard. If you played first base and Billy hit a ground ball on the infield, you'd better be sure your foot was only on the edge of the base when the throw came your way. Billy would just as soon step on your foot as on the base. When we watched him play, he was one of those teammates you felt lucky to have on your team. The other team no doubt wished he played on their team.

When my family moved to Kansas City, I lost track of him. Now all these years later, to find out that Billy Donahue has committed his life to God feels almost preposterous. I would have given better odds that he'd play major league baseball than devote his life to the Catholic Church.

"Really, Grandma? Billy Donahue is a Catholic priest? That's amazing."

"He was assigned to Our Lady of Guadalupe a few months ago. Go talk with him, Charlie. It can't hurt."

I'm still shaking my head. I don't know how talking to anyone about any of this is going to help.

"Please! Go! He'll be having Mass this morning."

"I don't know, Grandma. Talking to a priest this weekend certainly wasn't on my list of things to do. And Billy Donahue?"

As I continue to shake my head, I can see Grandma's eyes. They are pleading with me to go see him.

"Go! Get out of here."

Both of her hands are shooing me out of the house. Her eyes are encouraging. In fact, her look even seems hopeful. For me, that is the only sign of any hope in what seems like a hopeless situation. As far as I can tell, this marriage feels like it's on life support, and the air supply is slowly getting sucked out of it.

# 7

A Catholic church is precisely the last place I want to be on a Friday morning. I don't remember the last time I went to Mass.

Nora never missed going to Mass on Sunday. She grew up in a large Catholic family in central Wisconsin. Her father was a hardworking dairy farmer. Her mother had a tenacious family spirit. She was strong and passionate about her husband and children. Nora was the oldest of their five children. Their faith was the foundation of their very existence. Missing Mass on Sunday was never an option, even on the stark, dreary, freezing days of winter. A blowing, blinding blizzard could not keep the Sullivan family from finding their way to Mass.

My dad and mom raised my family in the Catholic faith, too. While Sunday Mass was a staple in grade school and through high school, I began to drift away in college. Meeting and dating Nora brought me back. After we were married the two of us were faithful to that obligation. But when weekends began demanding more time at work, I again began wandering away from the faith.

When my Sunday schedule permitted, the two of us would attend

Mass together. But those times were infrequent at best. This whole organized, seemingly manipulated do-this-don't-do-that religion "thing" really lost its luster when one Sunday a priest brought up what he called "the evil of contraception." I almost walked out. I was angry and offended. How could this man, much less a man who is not married, stand up there in front of God and give me a lecture about what I do in the privacy of my home? That was truly the end. I never went back.

If it weren't for my kind, thoughtful, insistent grandmother and the chance to see an old friend again, I wouldn't even consider stepping into a Catholic church. Our Lady of Guadalupe was founded in the early 1900s when immigrants from Mexico and other Central American countries trekked north to western Nebraska to work in the local beet factories. Our Lady of Guadalupe was opened to serve the growing Spanish-speaking population. All of us who grew up here knew it was a cultural cornerstone in the community.

The rain from last night has moved out. The morning sun is now squinting through a few tiny breaks in the low-hanging, ashen clouds. I feel as gloomy as this new day is gray. Pulling into the parking lot next to the modest, brick church, I can feel my stomach begin to roll and churn. I am tense and unsettled.

Thankfully, Mass is already over. My high school pal, still in his vestments, is walking down the front steps of the church to a small gathering area. He is chatting with his parishioners.

"Hola, Juan, ¿cómo está tu madre?"

"¡Mucho mejor! Gracias, Padre, por preguntarme."

"Seguimos rezando. ¿Bueno? Ten un día maravilloso."

Billy Donahue is a priest! My eyes aren't lying. Fr. Bill Donahue! I can hardly believe that this buddy I grew up with is a Catholic priest. Utterly shocking!

Slowing making my way to the front of the church, I can see this priest pal of mine from yesteryear still has that athletic build. He is tall and thin. His dark black hair loosely covers the top of his ears. He has a closely cropped beard. He is smiling and laughing with his parishioners.

"Gracias amigos. Nos vemos en la misa el domingo."

And where did he learn to speak Spanish?

As I move closer, he looks up and with a stunned, almost dumb-founded look recognizes me immediately.

"Charlie Landis! What in the world are you doing here?"

He throws his arms around me and nearly knocks the wind out of me with a big bear hug. Lifting me a few inches off the ground, he finally loosens his grip, stands back, and shakes his head in disbelief that these two friends have crossed paths again.

"What an incredible surprise! What brings you back? Is everybody okay?

"Yeah, everyone is fine. Just a weekend trip. It's been a while since I've seen my grandmother, and I thought this might be a good week-end to do that."

"Well, come inside. I've got a little bit of time before my first ap-pointment."

The last place I wanted to be today was *outside* a Catholic church. Now he's inviting me and taking me *inside*. Why do I have a feeling this gloomy day is only going to get gloomier?

"Charlie, come on in! We can sit here in a back pew. Let me go take off my vestments and I'll be right back."

As he heads to the sacristy behind the altar, the last few parishio-ners leave. As the door closes slowly behind them, I realize now that I'm the only one in the church. The quiet is startling. The absence of noise is actually a bit frightening. I can't remember the last time my little world didn't have someone or something vying for my time and attention.

"So, hey, God," I whisper somewhat cynically under my breath, "where are you? If you are real, why can't I hear you? No one else is here right now and so this is a great chance for you to say something."

Nothing!

"Come on, God! You've got my attention. It's just you and me. Say something."

Nothing!

Just what I thought! Not a word, Thanks, God...for nothing!

Billy is now making his way down the aisle to the back. He sits down.

"Man, it's great to see you."

"Same here, but I do have a question. What do I call you? Fr. Bill? Fr. Donahue? Bill? Billy?"

"Whatever you want. Most people around here call me Fr. Bill. Family and friends go back and forth between Bill and Billy. So, whatever is comfortable for you."

"You know, it's really quiet in here."

"Yeah, I love it. The silence is thunderous, isn't it?"

He laughs and continues, "This is where I come to get away from the distractions and noise of the world. I've discovered it's in the silence that I can really hear God."

"Really? I'm not sure I believe that. I mean I don't hear anything at all."

"Well, it can take some time to get quiet enough to listen and then hear him speak to your heart. It was St. Benedict who said that we have to learn how to listen to God by inclining what he called 'the ear of our heart.'"

Yeah, right! When did this guy get all religious and so enlightened?

"So, Charlie, tell me about yourself. Where are you living? What do you do? And tell me about your family."

"I have a law firm in Denver. It's pretty exciting right now. We're

37

negotiating a deal to merge our firm with another one in the San Francisco Bay area. It's an amazing time. It's going to set us on a solid financial foundation. The future is promising beyond anything I would have ever imagined. I was out west this past week finalizing the deal, and when I got to the Denver airport, almost on a whim before everything gets crazy busy at work, I thought it would be a good time to come back and see my grandmother. I had no idea it would include a reunion with you."

"A big time lawyer. That's terrific. And your family? Married, I presume?"

"Yes. Two children."

"Your wife? She has a name, right?"

Don't get too close, Billy. This is not what I want to talk about.

"Nora. The kids are twelve and ten. Robbie and Julie."

"How long have you two been married?"

"Oh gosh, what is it? Thirteen or fourteen years."

"Well, what is it? Thirteen? Or fourteen?"

As I do some quick math, I realize it's fifteen.

"Actually," as I try to laugh it off, "it's fifteen years. In fact, next month it will be sixteen."

I can tell Billy doesn't like the answer.

"Well, Charlie, with all due respect, I would tell you that you need to know how long you've been married. Whether you know it or not, your wedding day was the most important day of your life. That was the day when the two of you promised to love and honor each other for as long you both shall live. That was the day when you said 'yes' to one another to begin building your lives together, in the good times and the bad times, forever. You can't forget that."

Billy has put his Fr. Bill hat on. I knew this was a bad idea. I really have nothing to say to his scolding. He's right. I probably should know how long we've been married. But today I just don't care.

"So, Charlie, let me take a crazy guess as to why you're really here in Scottsbluff. I may be wrong, but something tells me you and Nora aren't doing too well these days. Listening to you as you talk about her, I can hear some hurt, maybe some anger and resentment, and the discouragement in your voice. My bet is that you decided to drive 200 miles north with the lame excuse of seeing your grandmother because this was easier than going home and dealing with what might be your broken marriage."

I don't know what to say. I have no words. I have no answers. Whatever I think I should say or want to say is being choked into a bedlam of emotions.

"Look, Charlie, I have to get to a meeting. But we have to continue the conversation. You probably don't want to do that, but I insist. Let's meet after lunch and continue this. Okay?"

My heart isn't in it, but I nod my head.

"Okay! There is a little drive-in restaurant over on 27th. It's called Scotty's. It'll be quiet and we can talk over a cup of coffee. About one o'clock. I'll see you there. Don't be late!"

His reassuring smile doesn't feel so reassuring. And how could he tell by my voice that Nora and I are having marriage problems?

**8**

Billy was right. It was much easier to travel four hours north to Scotts-bluff than go home and figure out how to cope with a shattered marriage. I need to think, find some space to get away, and ponder where all of this is heading. The better word to describe what I want to do is *escape*. Maybe my grandfather's log cabin can provide that. Grandma said she would leave it open.

The cabin sits about fifty yards behind the house. A gravel path winds its way through some large Douglas fir trees. The cabin is a little larger than a two-car garage and is snuggled among the hefty trees. The front porch is protected by a large overhanging roof. The door is extra wide, big, and heavy. Windows on both sides of the door reveal a rustic, inviting refuge.

I can see why Grandpa liked coming out here. An impressive stone fireplace takes up the back wall. A tan overstuffed leather chair sits off center in front of the hearth. It is large and no doubt amazingly comfortable. A small coffee table and standing lamp are nestled close by on the right.

A massive library of books takes up the entire right side of the cabin. What has to be hundreds of them fill a huge floor-to-ceiling bookcase. Did Grandma say this library was small? She's got to be kidding.

In the corner to the left of the door, two light blue wingback chairs sit on either side of a large, wooden drum table. An open Bible and the famous sculpted cowboy, the Bronco Buster by artist Frederic Remington, fill most of the surface.

Along the wall back toward the fireplace, a long sofa table holds a few books and two statues each about a foot tall. As I recall, one is the Sacred Heart of Jesus. The other one, the Immaculate Heart of Mary. To the right of the table, a doorway opens to a small bathroom and a kitchen-like area with a small refrigerator stashed beneath a counter. A coffee maker sits on top next to a half dozen neatly stacked mugs.

What's above the sofa table is probably why Grandma calls the cabin a shrine. A large pewter crucifix dominates this side of the cabin. It is surrounded by pictures and images of saints. Three small frames, each containing a quotation, have been positioned vertically near the right side of the table.

> "THOU HAST MADE US FOR THYSELF, O LORD, AND
> OUR HEART IS RESTLESS UNTIL IT FINDS ITS REST IN THEE."
> - SAINT AUGUSTINE

> "LET NOTHING PERTURB YOU, NOTHING FRIGHTEN YOU.
> ALL THINGS PASS. GOD DOES NOT CHANGE.
> PATIENCE ACHIEVES EVERYTHING."
> – SAINT TERESA OF AVILA

Right! God has great plans for me? I don't think so. In fact, I wonder anymore if God is even real. If there is a God out there, then where in the hell is he?

The Bible on the drum table is open to St. Paul's letter to the Ephesians, the fifth chapter. The heading reads *Wives and Husbands.* A few lines into it, the letter says,

*"Wives be subordinate to your husbands..."*

Well, there you go, Nora! Right there in the Bible, exactly what we need in this marriage to make it work. The anger and disillusionment begin to rise up again. I don't get it. What happened to us? Why doesn't she understand this? My big sigh of frustration is the only sound in the room.

Grandpa's bookcase is filled with a lot of religious books. I mean, a lot of them! Everything from the Catechism of the Catholic Church to the Didache, what looks to be a volume based on the teachings of the twelve Apostles. Perusing the titles, I see *The Confessions* by Saint Augustine, *Introduction to the Devout Life* by Saint Francis de Sales, *Dark Night of the Soul* by Saint John of the Cross, *Mere Christianity* by C.S. Lewis, *The Story of a Soul* by Saint Thérèse de Lisieux. Book after book by a lot of men and women who no doubt believe God is real, and I suspect would say they know him personally. Knowing God on any level in any way is simply an idea I cannot even begin to comprehend.

Glancing more carefully at the book titles, I come to the end of a row and notice a small leather volume with no title on the spine.

Pulling it out of the case, I see the word *Journal* embossed on the front.

"Oh, no," I whisper. "I wonder if this is Grandpa's journal."

I can't look at this. His personal, private thoughts about his life! Come on, Charlie, put it back. This is your grandfather probably writing down his most private thoughts. I can't read this! I put it back in its proper place on the shelf.

As I replace it in the bookcase, my attention turns to the other side of the cabin and the statue of Jesus. It feels like he's looking right at me, almost glaring into the depths of my soul. It's like he is saying, "You don't believe in me, do you?"

"No, Jesus, I don't think I do believe in you. If you are who you say you are, then where are you?"

The expression on his face looks forlorn, sad maybe. My emotions dig in. I can almost feel my heart harden. Nothing to say, Jesus? I didn't think so.

Another big sigh and I find myself looking again at Grandpa's leather journal. As I move back to the bookcase, I'm thinking that maybe just one page might be okay to read. What could it hurt? One page! No more, I promise myself. Opening it slowly to a page in the middle, I begin to read.

*Life is as dark right now as it has ever been. The darkness is stifling, suffocating, paralyzing. I feel like I am in a cave deep underground where light cannot possibly exist. I cannot see up... or down. Or to the right or to the left. All I can feel are the bottoms of my feet, but I have no idea if the surface I'm standing on is the size of a football field or a tiny square tile.*

*My fear is mortifying. It seems my feet are nailed to whatever I might be standing on. I am afraid to step forward or backward or side to side because I don't know if any step in any direction will toss me into a deep pit or throw me off a steep cliff.*

*So, I stand motionless. The only thing I can hear is my rapid* breathing. If I listen closely enough I can hear and feel the feeble thumping of my petrified heart.

This darkness is beyond any blackness I could have ever imagined. It is dense and gagging and crushing. I find myself squinting, almost forcing my eyes to see something, anything that might give me some hope, some sense that there is something in this dark world that surrounds me.

Couldn't there be even a teeny, miniscule pinprick of light somewhere? Something – anything – that says there might be an end to this world of darkness? It really seems as if this realm is a world of absence where nothing exists but me, my fears… my terror actually!

This horror is overpowering, which only feeds the loneliness and the stark reality of the darkness.

Alone! No one! My only companion is the darkness!

Any hope for anyone or anything is gone! Extinguished! Dead!

The hopelessness is inching its way into despair.

In a moment of sheer desperation, I yell, "Is anyone out there? Can anyone hear me?"

Darkness has a way of not answering. Darkness swallows up the sound. It doesn't know how to give anything back, even a slight echo or a small, ever-so-tiny scratch of light.

Darkness doesn't talk. Darkness is too big. Darkness doesn't care.

I wonder if this is what hell is like. An eternity of darkness.

I thought hell was all about fire. At least, with fire there is light. But not here. Not in this dark, dark blackness.

There is nothing! No gleam! No glow! No hope!

Just me! Alone! Forever!

Life has never been so heavy, so daunting, and so dark.

Gently closing the journal, I am stunned. What in the world could this kind Nebraska rancher have been going through? On top of that, I had no idea anyone anywhere else in the world could ever experience darkness like I am. I don't understand how in the midst of a successful law firm, working with a lot of people doing great things, with so many friends, with children and a wife, how I could feel so isolated. And yet, I do. This aloneness is haunting and making the choices in front of me terrifying and increasingly foreboding.

# 9

Scotty's is a small drive-in diner on the east side of Scottsbluff. As I ease through the front door, Billy-Bill-Fr. Bill-or-whatever-the-heck-I-should-call-him is standing at the counter placing an order. The creaky sound of the door opening turns his attention my way.

"Hey, Charlie. thanks for coming. Coffee? I'm buying."

"Sure. You bet. Black."

"Grab a booth in back and I will be right there."

Sliding into one of the wooden booths near the back, I'm tense and not looking forward to where this conversation might be heading. But it will be good to catch up. Hopefully this won't get too personal. Billy is paying, grabbing the two mugs, and heading my way. As he sets our coffee down and settles into the booth, I find myself thinking again that I still can't fathom the notion that Billy Donahue is a priest.

"So, Charlie, how are you? And is that your Porsche?"

With a slight smile, I nod my head.

"Nice ride! A big-time lawyer, for sure, if you can afford that. Wow! So, hey, I can't believe you're here."

"Yeah, I can't either. But you were right about Nora. It's just a tough time right now. I needed some time and a little space to sort some of this out. This big deal with my law firm has been all-consuming. I know the coming weeks at work are going to be insane. With all of that and trying to figure out what's going on in the marriage, it seemed to make some sense to come back. So, here I am."

Billy wants to say something. But I don't let him get the words out of his mouth.

"But enough about me! How are you? I keep thinking I can't really believe you are a priest. So, how did my friend Wild Bill Donahue become Fr. Bill Donahue?"

"To be honest, there are times when I can't believe it either. But I think it's another great illustration that God has a really wicked sense of humor."

We both chuckle a bit. He pauses and looks down at his coffee. As he slowly stirs it with his spoon, a slight smile seems to confirm his lifelong choice.

"But, Charlie, I have to tell you. It all feels so right. I truly believe it's exactly what I'm supposed to be doing. I realized years ago that God really does have a plan for me. For all of us, really. You, too, Charlie, as a husband to Nora and a father to your kids. But for me, after years of running away from God, I discovered that life is all about serving God and others, those people he places in my life. For me, that happens to be as a priest in his Church."

"Running away? What do you mean you were running away from God?"

"You really want to hear the story?"

"Sure!"

Actually, I'm thinking, let's talk about anything but Nora or me or what's going on in my life.

"Well, after high school I went to San Diego State on a baseball scholarship. I had scholarship offers at other schools much closer to home. But San Diego! How could anyone not want to go to southern California to play baseball? My parents finally agreed that I could go there on one condition. I had to promise I would find a way to get to Mass on Sunday. So, I figured I could give up an hour a week to go to southern California and play baseball."

"Well, Billy, that sounds like a pretty good deal."

"That's what I thought. So, I get there and find the campus Newman Center. I meet a few people. Some become really good friends and they ask me to be part of their weekend Mission Team, where they help serve the poor across the border in Tijuana. I'm thinking to myself that's not part of the agreement with my dad and mom. Mission trips to Tijuana is going to go far beyond my commitment to go to Mass on Sunday. Besides, I tell these new friends, I'm on a baseball scholarship, and I won't have time for any weekend excursions south of the border."

"And the baseball excuse gets you out of that? Probably not, right?"

"Yeah, they all pointed out that playing baseball was not a year-round commitment. It was close to year-round, but they were right. I was going to have a few free weekends So, on those weekends when I wasn't practicing or playing, we all got into a big old, beat-up gray van that seemed to have more rust spots than paint. It seemed like it needed a quart of oil about every 50 miles, but it ran. And off we'd go to Tijuana. Twenty-five miles of chugging and lurching south into Mexico. We laughed a lot about what God seemed to be asking all of us to do. I have to tell you, Charlie, it was life-changing. I had no idea there was that kind of poverty in the world."

"Really? How so?"

"As you probably know, Tijuana sits on the border. The crossing from Mexico into San Diego is said to be the busiest land crossing in the world. Some estimates say over the course of a year one hundred million people cross over the border. But the poor who live there are some of the poorest anywhere in the world. We saw people living in cardboard boxes. Many didn't have or couldn't get a decent job. The drugs were everywhere and destroying so many lives. The kids spent most of their days on the street begging. Some would hang around across the street from outdoor restaurants. When the customers would pay their bills and leave, the kids would swoop in like birds to grab any leftover food on the plates. As they ran away, they were shoving the food into their mouths like they had never eaten and might never eat again. It was so incredibly sad to see that. We would spend most of our time working to help provide food and clothing. Some weekends were spent simply trying to find people a hot shower. Some hadn't had a hot shower in months. But as tough as it was to see the people in those conditions, I really began to fall in love with them. They had simply been born into a world that hadn't been too kind to them. I often wondered why I was born here in Scottsbluff and not in some poor part of the world like Tijuana. I knew I had been truly blessed and found myself wanting to give back in some way. So, I kept going on those trips. It was where I first started to learn and speak Spanish."

"And the priesthood? How did that happen?"

"You really want to know, huh?"

"Yeah, I do. I mean if you asked any of us in high school who was most likely to be a priest, it wouldn't have been you. Trust me, there's no way it would have been you. No way!"

"Yeah, I get that."

Billy is now leaning back in the booth, looking down at his coffee cup, and beginning to smile a bit more. It seems as if he is traveling back in time recalling something he is not quite sure he wants to tell me. Then with a quiet sigh, he looks up, leans forward, and begins.

"I think I knew for a long time that God might be calling me to be a priest. I don't really know if I just didn't *want* to do it or I didn't think I *could* do it. But there were more than a few times when we served the school Masses at St. Agnes that I began to get some sense that maybe being a priest was something I should consider. I really can't explain it completely, but something deep inside of me was telling me that one day I would be a priest. Not *might* be a priest, but that I *would* be a priest."

"What do you mean by 'deep inside?'"

"Well, Charlie, like I said, it's hard to explain. It wasn't exactly a voice, but as I think back on those days, it was something like that. It was some sense of awareness or maybe a premonition that said very clearly to me that I would become a priest. It happened so often that I got to the point where I didn't want to serve Mass anymore. But Father just kept asking. Besides, it got me out of that math class I had trouble with. I couldn't decide if dealing with fractions was easier than dealing with God."

"What grade was that? And this was going on while the two of us were serving Mass together?"

"Yeah, you were there. It started near the end of seventh grade. You were still in sixth. Then for me it all became fairly intense through most of eighth grade."

"What did you do?"

Billy laughs out loud and the grin on his face gets bigger. His eyes are full of life.

"I started running."

"What do you mean you 'started running?'"

"Well, come on, Charlie! I mean, I'm a year away from high school and girls and baseball. How could being a priest be more important than that? The truth is I was pretty scared and didn't know what to do with this idea of someday being a priest. I didn't tell anyone. Not my parents. Not my friends. Certainly not anyone at church. So, I get to high school and suddenly the girls and the parties and the drinking are a lot more fun than thinking about the priesthood."

I laugh out loud. "And the nickname, Wild Bill Donahue, was born. I have to tell you that a lot of Monday mornings were filled with stories of the weekend escapades of Billy Donahue."

We are both laughing at the memories. We have wandered back to a time when we were much younger and maybe naïve about the futures we would face.

"Whether all of those stories were actually true is up for debate. But I can tell you, Charlie, what is true is much of high school was really an attempt to ignore or run away from this 'thing' called the priesthood. And I probably did a pretty good job of doing that."

"How so?"

"I think I was just scared. Was I really hearing God? Was he really asking me or telling me that I would be a priest? It seemed like some deep fear was gripping, almost strangling my heart. Going to church in those days was tough. After a while I sort of felt like I was being dragged there by my parents. I went, but I didn't want much to do with it. When I started high school, baseball became more important. Then when it looked like I could get pretty good at it, I was all in. Summer traveling teams, more batting practice, and an all-out assault on getting into the best shape of my life. By the time I was a senior, a lot of college coaches began calling with scholarship offers and the priest 'thing' really went away. So, I accepted the offer to San Diego State and played baseball for four years."

"So, when did the priest 'thing' walk back into your life?"

"Well, the weekend mission trips into Tijuana pulled me deeper into my faith. The people and the poverty they had to live with put a face on the suffering Christ. These people had names. They were moms and dads and brothers and sisters. I got to know a lot of them. When I would come back to campus to my nice life, I was simply heartbroken that so many families were living in such stark poverty. I wanted to do something. I wanted to do more than I was doing. I wasn't sure what that meant, but the experience made a big impression on me. As touched as I was by all of that, I wasn't thinking anything about the priesthood. But during my senior year, I was with some friends one weekend and we ended up in a local bar a few blocks off campus. It was a little before two o'clock in the morning and the bar was about to close. The bartender, as all bartenders do when the bar is about to shut down, began shouting, 'Last call! Last call!' But what I heard was 'Last call, Billy! Last call, Billy!' I knew in that moment that God hadn't given up on me. I had no doubt that God was speaking to me through that bartender and that he was very directly and very personally calling me to be one of his priests."

"You really knew?"

"Yeah, I did. In Luke's Gospel we hear the story about the two disciples on the road to Emmaus and after their encounter with Jesus they said, '…were not our hearts burning when He talked to us.' I heard those words – 'Last call, Billy! Last call, Billy!' – and my heart was on fire. I knew exactly what I needed to do."

"So, what did you do?"

"The short story is that I had to tell my girlfriend first. We were pretty serious about our relationship and had even talked about getting married. But she was great. She had a strong faith and understood that it was about God's plan, not her plan or even my plan. She jokingly said one time that if I really was being called to be a priest, she didn't want to be the one standing in the way of God. So, I finished my senior year at San Diego State, came back home, told my parents I thought I was being called to be a priest and wanted to go to the seminary to find out for sure. So, I went, was ordained, and was initially assigned to a parish in Grand Island, which included teaching Spanish to the ninth and tenth graders at Central Catholic.

Then a few months ago, the bishop reassigned me to be the pastor here at Our Lady of Guadalupe. But enough about me! Let me get some refills. I want to hear about you and Nora."

As Billy slides out of the booth, I know that I'm about to wade into a murky, dark pool of water that might have no bottom. I am not expecting this to be a good conversation.

# 10

Billy comes back to the table and sets down our two cups of coffee. He carefully pushes mine back in front of me. "So, how are you doing?"

"Well, for the most part pretty good. This merger deal in California is really big. I would have never imagined anything like this happening to what I figured would always be a small law firm in Denver. But about five years ago, a friend of mine in New Jersey asked me if I'd be interested in helping him file a malpractice lawsuit against a doctor who, during surgery on a middle-aged man, mistakenly took out the wrong lung. The sheer incompetency and utter arrogance of this doctor was stunning. So, we filed the suit and ended up winning a twenty-million-dollar settlement. The case put us on the map, so to speak. We started getting more phone calls and began taking on more medical error lawsuits. We were winning a lot of eight-and-nine-figure cases. As we grew larger, other firms began inquiring about merging and opening offices in other parts of the country. I had a lot of offers, but the California deal felt right and seemed to work for all of us. We think we can open a New York office within the next three years and an office in London within five years. The final papers get signed next week. It's going to be a big, big deal."

"So, Charlie, with all due respect, when I asked the question about how you're doing, I meant how are you and Nora doing?

Damn! Here we go! As I reach for my coffee and take a sip, I'm thinking I could say I don't want to talk about it, slip out of the booth, and leave. At the same time I'm fairly confident Billy would get up, follow me outside, and not let me avoid him or the situation.

"Not good!"

I could tell from the serious, patient, I've-got-all-day look on his face that my two-word answer was not good enough.

"I don't know where to start."

"That's okay. Just start."

"It's not the same. We are different people today. I have my interests. Nora has hers. I have this important job that takes a lot of hours. She has the kids and her friends. I do what I want. She does what she wants. We are like two strangers living in the same house. It's all so different. We barely talk to each other anymore. When we do talk, it seems to be about the kids or some news event or complaining about things that don't matter, like the weeds in a neighbor's yard. Today is nothing like when we first met and started dating. Those days were full of fun and laughter. These days aren't so much fun, and the most laughter in the house seems to be on a laugh track of something we hear on television. I'm not sure we even look at each other much anymore. It's a very dark time right now. A lot of sleepless nights wondering about how to get out of this."

"So, you want to get out of the marriage? You're really thinking about getting a divorce?"

I look back down at the coffee mug and realize the finality of where the conversation is going.

"Yeah, I think I want a divorce."

"What does Nora want?"

"She probably doesn't want a divorce, but I think I'll be better off. I think she'll be better off, too."

"And what about the kids? Do you think they will want their mom and dad to get a divorce?"

"Probably not, but kids are resilient. They'd be okay."

"Don't be so sure. Divorce will scar them for the rest of their lives. You can try to ignore the truth of that, but don't be delusional about what will happen to them when they see their dad give up on their mom. Trust me, if they see you give up on your wife, they will wonder if you plan some day on giving up on them, too. So, what about those marriage vows you made to one another on your wedding day? You know, promising to honor one another all the days of your life in the good times and in the bad times?"

"Come on, Billy! Things change. People change. That was a long time ago."

"So, let me see if I understand what you are saying. Marriage is for the rest of your lives or sixteen years, whichever comes first."

My clenched teeth and tight jaw are fighting to extinguish the small fire of anger beginning to well up inside of me. He has no idea what I'm going through. Walk in my shoes for a while, Buddy Boy! You'd see how tough this is!

"Is there another woman?"

His question shocks me back into the moment.

"No, there is not 'another woman.' I could never do that to Nora."

"But you could divorce her? That would be okay, right?"

I don't have an answer.

"So, when you were married, what did you expect your life would be like?"

"Not this!"

56

Billy leans back in the booth, takes a sip of coffee, and looks at me with what seems to be some sense of understanding and compassion.

"Look, Charlie, life gets complicated. Every relationship goes through ups and downs. It's a roller coaster at times. Huge highs and low lows. It's then a question of what are you going to do when life gets difficult and heads in a direction you hadn't planned on."

"Well, this low is pretty low and I don't see how we make our way through this."

"Okay! But back to my question – what did you expect when you were married?"

"I guess I expected we would be happy. And trust me, this marriage is nothing close to happy."

"So, Charlie, what is happy? A good friend in the seminary would ask that question all the time. What is happy? Most people tend to put a dollar sign on their answer. A high-paying job. A big home. A nice car. And look, Charlie, you have all of that. But you're not happy, are you? No, you're not. You probably don't want to hear this, but real happiness will only be found in God. The foundation of that reality is your marriage and family. But you will probably have to figure that one out for yourself."

Billy is waiting for a response I don't really have. How do I find happiness in something I don't even know is real?

"So, back to Nora. How did the two of you meet?"

The question surprises me and takes me immediately back to that moment I first saw Nora. Time seems to rush back to those days when life was good and carefree and all about the two of us.

"My family had moved to Kansas City right after my senior year in high school. For college they wanted and encouraged me to stay close to home. When the Army gave me an ROTC scholarship to Creighton University in Omaha, we decided since that was less than three hours away, that would be close enough. The plan was to get an undergraduate degree and go to law school. I met Nora the fall of my junior year."

A deep feeling of nostalgia begins to creep into our conversation. Those days were magical.

"It wasn't a very romantic moment at all. I like to say we met by accident. Literally! I was riding my motorcycle through campus on a drizzly morning, the pavement was wet, and I slid into the rear end of her little red Chevy. Neither of us was hurt and the damage to her car and my bike was minor. But she was furious. She was very, very cute and very, very furious. Her first words to me were, 'What the hell were you doing?' I don't remember what I said, but was she cute or what? I was infatuated right away. We exchanged the insurance information and I asked for her campus address and phone number. In case, I needed to stay in touch, of course! We went our separate ways, but I called her a few days later just to be sure she was okay and the insurance was taking care of the repairs. She said it was all taken care of. Then I took a big breath and asked her out. I told her I wasn't too proud of the way we met, but wondered if I could buy her lunch one day to help make up for what I had done. And she said yes! I couldn't believe it, but that was the beginning of Charlie and Nora. We met at the library the next Saturday morning, studied for a while, and went to lunch after that."

"So, you were a junior. What year was Nora?"

"Nora was a sophomore. We ended up getting pretty serious pretty quickly. We dated three years and were married after she graduated. I ended up in an accelerated program to get my law degree in two years. That first year after we were married we rented a small, wood frame house off campus. The doors wouldn't shut all the way, the floors squeaked, and the basement was as creepy as anything I'd ever seen. I was honestly afraid to go down the steps. But hey, we had each other! When I finished school, I took a job at a small law firm in Denver. To meet my ROTC scholarship obligation I was assigned to the office of the Judge Advocate General, the JAG office at Headquarters of the Colorado Army National Guard. After a few years with the law firm, I decided to go out on my own and open a small law office. As scary as that was, it seemed to work. I kept busy and made enough money to support Nora and our two small children. A year or so after that, I won that big malpractice suit and life changed quickly. A lot of recognition in the media, more money, new cars, a bigger house, and the beginning of what I could say has turned into a very successful career. It was all sort of amazing the way everything fell together."

"So, what was she like? When you first met Nora, what was so special about her?"

The memories of that misty day in Omaha, the accident, and those wonder-filled days at Creighton are as vivid as if they had just happened.

"Nora was incredible. Just as cute as she could be. Short brown hair, the friendliest of smiles that seemed to light up her big brown eyes. Great looking legs, by the way! And we had fun. A lot of fun. We laughed a lot and had so many good times. I remember those days like they were yesterday."

"Where did she grow up?"

"Marshfield, Wisconsin. It's a small town in the middle of the state. Her dad is a dairy farmer. Her mom helps work the farm. She has two brothers and two sisters. Nora is the oldest. A very Catholic family and even today Nora is still a bit of a fanatic about her faith."

"Well, Charlie, is 'fanatic' the right word? You make it sound like she has some crazy ideas about living out her faith. With all due respect, I might suggest using the word 'passionate' or 'devoted.'"

"Yeah, 'fanatical' or 'passionate' or 'devoted' would pretty much describe her."

All of those warm-hearted memories of our times at Creighton and those first simple years in Denver have suddenly been washed away in a flash flood of anger and contempt. Billy is not saying anything. The look on his face seems to border on something between empathy and disdain. I can't tell which.

"Look, Charlie, I have to watch my time. I have another appointment I will need to get to. But let's grab another cup of coffee. I have two more questions for you."

Two more questions! Is this grilling ever going to end?

# 11

"So, what happened? When did this marriage of yours begin to head south?"

"I don't know for sure. Looking back it all seems sort of gradual. After a few years things started to change. I had my job. Nora had the kids. It seemed like we had two separate lives. It was like I had to take care of working and making money. She took care of everything around the house. We seemed to be heading in different directions and wanting to do different things. I had my guy friends. We played a lot of softball during the summer and basketball during the winter. She did her thing with her girlfriends. After a while, if I'm going to be honest, it just seemed like she didn't care about me anymore."

"How is your sex life?"

I am taken aback by the question. I didn't think we'd get this personal.

"Gosh, Billy! A bit personal, don't you think?"

"Yeah, I do think it's personal. But if I'm going to help, this conversation needs to get personal. So, how is your sex life?"

My throat is getting tighter. Okay, put it out there. If he wants to know, then here it is.

"It's not very good. Routine is probably a good description. Predictable! No spontaneity! Lifeless! Matter-of-fact! Something married couples do every once in a while and so every once in a while we do it. We have sex. Mostly it seems reserved for birthdays and anniversaries. Any passion we ever had is a distant memory. Nothing like when we were first married. I remember one time that Nora said she felt used. I hated hearing that, but I could understand it. So, our sex life is not exactly setting our sheets on fire."

"You know, Charlie, none of that is unusual. Any relationship goes through the ups and downs of life. Married couples especially begin to get pulled in so many different directions that it is difficult to stay focused on each other and what you want and hope your life will be like. Jobs, kids, and money all get in the way of the two of you. When you were married, you promised each other that you would love each other in the good times and the bad times. I like to remind couples that you don't make those vows to one another because bad times *might* happen. Bad times *do* happen. The question then is what are you going to do when the bad times punch you in the gut and smack you in the face? A lot of couples give up and run away from each other. In good marriages, couples fight for the marriage and learn to work through those times, which happen in all marriages."

"I don't know, Billy. This is pretty dark stuff right now. I don't see how we're going to get through it. I think it's time to say it's not working and figure out a way to move on with our lives."

Billy is quiet, maybe waiting for me to say something else. But I'm done. Enough personal crud!

"When did things begin to change for you and Nora? It's not always the case, but a lot of times there is a moment in a marriage when what each of you wants suddenly and powerfully collides with what the other person wants. One wants one thing and the other one wants something completely different. Life just blows up. Did something like that happen to the two of you?"

"Maybe!"

Billy's question throws me back to a moment about three years ago.

"A few years ago we ended up having some pretty heated discussions."

My words trail off as I think about the big fight that perhaps signaled the impending death of our marriage. I had pushed those arguments aside and buried them in a deep, dark cavern of my life. I didn't want to talk about it then and I don't want to talk about it now.

"What happened?"

"Damn, Billy! Do we have to do this?"

"Maybe we don't *have* to do this. But if you're looking for me to agree with you that divorce is okay and is the only option for you and Nora, that's not going to happen. This is a fight. And I'm here to put on the gloves with you and fight for you and Nora. Marriage is too important for you to just give up and throw your life away. So, what happened?"

I can tell this friend-turned-priest is serious. As much as I want to walk out, I know I can't do that.

"Nora wanted more children!"

"And you didn't?"

"No, why would I? We had two already. As they say, a boy for me and a girl for her. I mean, the added expense, the time to take care of them, and more children would take time away from all the other things in our life. I didn't want the responsibility, and besides, my job was taking more time. I didn't need more kids to interfere with a career that was beginning to take off."

"Why did Nora want more children?"

"As I said, she grew up in a very Catholic family. After we were married for a few years, she began reading more about contraception and why the Catholic Church is against it. Since we had been told during our engagement that the decision to use contraception was up to our own consciences, the two of us agreed that birth control would be okay. After we had Robbie and Julie, she kept taking the pill. But she started to have some side effects and wanted to get off of it. Nothing serious, I didn't think."

"But maybe not, right? It might have been more serious than you thought?"

"Well, she said she wasn't feeling well. She noticed her face was breaking out. Her doctor detected a small spike in her blood pressure. And she complained about feeling a bit depressed. That's when she started reading more about what the Church really taught about contraception. An 'intrinsic evil' is what she said the Church called it. She had a lot of questions but said she thought we should consider having more kids. I told her absolutely not. The conversations turned into a long series of intense arguments. Lots of yelling from me. Lots of tears from Nora. She was also upset and angry because I didn't seem to care about the side effects and what was happening to her body. We simply quit talking about it. Looking back, I can see that maybe that's where the marriage began falling apart. But here we are! It's time to move on. This is not going to get fixed."

Billy is pensive. He seems to be weighing his words carefully.

"Let me be sure I understand. You don't think high blood pressure and depression are serious? And you think it's okay for your wife to put a bunch of chemicals into her body every day?"

I'm struggling to keep my growing anger at bay. My fists begin to clench.

"I suppose I never looked at it that way."

"With all due respect, Charlie, that's exactly what you're asking her to do. As Nora's husband, whether you believe it or not, you have an obligation to uphold her dignity. You're not doing that. Your sexual relationship, your love making, creates a bond, a closeness that certainly provides pleasure, but also offers the possibility of new life. That's God's plan for the two of you. But contraception short circuits that divine plan. You are putting some "thing" between the two of you and God. If you'll be honest with yourself, Charlie, you want to have sex whenever you want without the responsibility that you might have a baby. I would point out that's a pretty selfish outlook on what a sexual relationship should be like. It's really all about you, isn't it? Nora has effectively become an object. She is not a wife for you to love, but a tool for you to grab when your libido needs some attention. No wonder she said she felt used."

Billy's voice is getting more emphatic.

"Have you ever read the volumes of fine print inserted in a package of birth control pills? Probably not, right?"

My voice is a shallow mumble. "No, I haven't!"

"So, here's the reality. This so-called pill is a mixture of chemicals that dramatically alter a woman's natural cycle. What God has created in a woman's body is now being manipulated by these man-made chemicals. And that can be dangerous! Not to you, because you're not taking the pill. But to Nora, it can be a very different story. These pharmaceutical companies will tell you they believe their pills are safe and any complications are rare. But then in an insert with thousands of words that unfolds into a sheet of paper about eighteen inches long, they tell you what might go wrong. They list things like heart attacks, strokes, blood clots, liver tumors, and, oh yeah, even death. Some research indicates now that the pill is associated with breast cancer. Why then would you want your wife to put that kind of thing into her body? It doesn't hurt you. But it can do a lot of harm to the woman you promised to love and honor all the days of your life."

Billy takes a big breath. He seems to realize he's raising his voice and needs to settle down.

"But come on, Billy. Everyone uses birth control."

"Well, that's not true. Not everyone uses birth control. I work with a good number of couples who don't contracept. They struggle at times, but for all sorts of reasons they have made the decision not to use birth control and trust God in all areas of their marriage. Because here's the thing about birth control. Using contraception effectively takes God out of your life as a married couple. God is great as long as he stays out of your bedroom. Hey, Lord, help me at work, guard our children, keep us safe on our weekend trips, but see that door to our bedroom, you, God, stay on the other side. You can't come in. You're not welcome. That's the evil part of contraception. It's taking the first Commandment 'to love the Lord thy God will all thy heart, with all thy soul, and with all thy mind' and telling him you'll love him with only part of you. Not all of you and, by the way, nothing below the belt."

I smile at the comment. But his message is not going unnoticed.

"Here's the other thing that most people don't know about contraception. Until the early 1930s, every church in the world viewed contraception as an intrinsic evil. Every single one! Then the Anglican church changed its teaching so that individual couples could decide for themselves whether to use birth control. That opened the door. One by one, every Christian church in the world eventually adopted that same stance."

Billy pauses and holds up his index finger to make a point.

"Every Christian church in the world relaxed its teaching except one. The Catholic Church! We are the only church that still calls it what it is – an intrinsic evil. It's not always a popular teaching, but it's the truth and it's been that way for two thousand years. All part of God's plan from the beginning. Which brings me to my second question. Where is God in your life?"

"Well, that's a pretty big question. Let me use the restroom first. Coffee in, coffee out, you know."

As I get up from the booth, I know I need a break from this incessant cross-examination. What I really want to tell him is that he has no business lecturing me about what I should be doing or not doing in our bedroom. He's a priest for God's sake. What the hell does he know? This reunion is nothing like I thought it would be.

# 12

"So, where is God in your life?"

I take a big breath and let it out slowly. "I'm not sure."

"What do you mean you're not sure? Here's the truth, Charlie. We all have a god. As I listen to you, it seems to me that your god right now is this deal you're putting together on the West Coast. Which is all about money or power or prestige or probably all three. Those are the gods that begin with a small 'g' and those gods are what get you out of bed in the morning and drive you to succeed. All so you can make more money or get more authority or get some sense of self-importance. All of us have those gods in our life. For a lot of people, those gods are the only ones that matter and end up driving God, our Creator, into a dark hole. And we call him out only when we are in trouble. So, tell me, the God that begins with a big 'G,' where is he in your life?"

"I don't know. I don't see him doing much."

"You don't see God working in your life? Nora, your children, your home, all of your material possessions are all gifts from God. You don't see that?"

"Maybe, but I don't see God giving that to me. It's taken a lot of hard work to get here."

Billy pauses, pondering and letting that sink in. He seems perplexed.

"Then let me ask about your prayer life. How is that?"

"I guess I pray sometimes. Not a lot!"

"Might I guess that if you pray, you're asking God for something you want, right?"

"Probably."

"And might I guess that if God answers that prayer, you look at it as something you did and not God answering that prayer, right?"

"Probably."

"See, Charlie, this is normally how this goes. You pray to God and if things go your way, then it's something you did. If things don't go the way you want them to go, then it's God's fault. I take it you're probably not going to church much."

"No, I'm not. Sunday Mass is not for me anymore. Nora gets pretty upset when I don't go. She tells me over and over that I'm setting a bad example for the kids."

"Which, by the way, you are. Whether you realize it or not, your kids are watching you closely. Was going to church for you always this way?"

"No! When we were first married, we never missed Mass on Sunday. Then after a few years I started missing here and there. Sort of drifting away, I guess, when my job started taking more time. A few nights a week I had to stay to get some things done and get a head start on the next day. Then I began going in on Saturdays and Sundays. Nora and the kids would still get to Mass on Sunday, but I didn't have a lot of extra time for that. God sort of became unreal to me.

Almost like he wasn't there anymore. If he was ever there to begin with!"

"You know, Charlie, I heard a good number of years ago that if you don't feel close to God, you have to ask yourself the question, 'Who moved?' If you don't feel close to God, it's not because he walked away from you. You walked away from him. That would be your choice, not his. It sounds like that's what you did and are still doing. Walking away from God."

I don't have an answer for that. I do know that God, if he is real, is not playing a big part in my life. I can't see him. I can't hear him. I can't touch him.

"So, Charlie, you're probably thinking that you can't see him or hear him or even touch him, and I get that. But here is the truth about God. God is real or he is not. It's that simple. Jesus is who he says he is or he is not. Now here's the truth of all that – one day both of us are going to find out if God is real. Either I am right and you are wrong, or you are right and I am wrong. No gray areas here. It's all black and white. There's no in-between. A quote from C.S. Lewis, which I memorized a long time ago, always gives me pause to recognize the truth of who the Lord is in my life.

*"A man who was merely a man and said the sort of things Jesus said would not be a great moral teacher. He would either be a lunatic – on the level with the man who says he is a poached egg – or else he would be the devil of hell. You must make your choice. Either this man was, and is, the Son of God, or else a madman or something worse."*

"I happen to think Jesus is not simply a great moral teacher or a lunatic or a poached egg. I believe that Jesus is the Messiah whom prophets pointed to throughout the Old Testament, the only Begotten Son of God, the Christ who gave his life for you and for me and rose from the dead. Now you might not believe that, but here is the

70

reality of God – one day in this life we will all take a final breath. We don't know when that is going to happen, but that day will be our last day here on earth. It will be at that precise moment that we will all find out if God is who he says he is. Right now, based on what you're telling me, one day one of us is going to be bitterly disappointed. To say it again, God is real…or he is not."

"Yeah, yeah, Billy, but I'm just not into organized religion."

"I hear that from a lot of people. I'm not sure I know exactly what that means."

"You know, all the rules and regulations. Do this! Don't do that! Go to church! Be a goody-goody holy Joe."

"I think saying that you're not into 'organized religion' is just an excuse not to go to church. I think in the end some people, maybe you, believe that Christianity is too hard, that living a life of faith can sometimes be too demanding. Christianity is all about loving others. Sometimes, for all of us, it's easier to think only about ourselves. It's a me-first mentality. It's all about what I want to do, where I want to go, what I want to watch on TV. It's not about what's best for some-one else who happens to cross my path. We then begin to ignore the people who might need a helping hand. We treat the people we work with poorly. We snap at our loved ones because they might be inter-rupting what we want to do. With all due respect, Charlie, it sounds like it might be easier for you not to go church. Not to be with Nora and the kids. I suspect it's easier to get up on a Sunday morning, put on some jeans and a sweatshirt and go to work. It's easier to say 'yes' to some friends who want you to play golf on Sunday morning. You say 'yes' to them, but 'no' to God and your family. All of that is easier and more convenient than making God a priority and spending a day with your wife and children."

"Yeah, but if I don't work on weekends, I'm not going to be able to finish all of the things I have to do. This deal with the California group doesn't happen if I don't work nights and weekends."

"I think if you gave God what was due to God, you'd find a whole lot of time to get everything done. But you would have to try to see for yourself if that's true. And you say you're not into 'organized religion!' You know what? I am not into that either."

"What do you mean you're not into 'organized religion?' You have to be. You're a priest."

"That's right. I am a priest, who is not into 'organized religion.' What I am into is Jesus Christ. He asks me to do some things. So, I try to do them. I follow the rules and regulations not because I love the rules and regulations, but because I love Jesus. Let's be honest. All of life, every part of it, is about rules and regulations. That's what gives us structure and order. Without rules and regulations, our lives would be messier than they already are. Take baseball, for example. The rules and regulations tell us that we get three strikes to try to hit the ball. You don't stand in the batter's box and tell the umpire you're changing the rules and you want four strikes. It doesn't work that way. That's not how the game is played. You follow the rules of baseball not because you love the rules. You follow the rules because you love the game. It's the same with the Church. You follow the rules not because you love the rules, but because you love the man who started it. And it was Jesus who said if you want to be happy, then follow me. He tells us that he will show us the way. So, we follow him because we love him. It's the same thing in marriage. You live out your marriage vows not because it's easy, but because you love the person you promised your life to. That doesn't mean you always *like* the other person. But you are called to love her, to think of her first, to put her needs and wants before what you think you need and what you want. You promised to love her even in these difficult days you're facing right now."

"Difficult is probably not the right word, Billy. Whatever that means, it's more difficult than that. I never saw any of this coming. I never dreamed our life would be falling apart like this."

"So, Charlie, lots of things to think about. But before I get going, here's one more thing to ponder. I do hear what you're saying. You haven't said it directly, but it's obvious that you are angry, upset, and probably afraid of what you think is in front of you. I suspect you want it all to change."

Billy is right about that. But I don't know how to change any of this.

"Here's the truth about change. Change begins with you. If you want things to change in your life, Charlie has to change Charlie first. When you begin to make other people in your life more important than yourself, then everything else begins to change, too. Trust me, there is a freedom in that reality. Think about that time in your life when you and Nora first met. Back then it was all about her, wasn't it? You wanted to make things right for her first. So, you took her to nice places. You probably got dressed up. I might guess you even wrote her notes. You couldn't wait to see her. It might be a bit corny, but it's called romance. You were trying to tell her how important she was to you. It was all about making her happy first. You didn't care about yourself all that much. It's in those moments we find true freedom."

Billy looks right at me with a long, intense stare to help emphasize his point. I'm not so sure I believe what he is saying. But he is right about those early days of our life at Creighton. I couldn't wait to see her. I found myself making up excuses to be around her. These days I find myself making up excuses *not* to be around her.

"Okay, Charlie, I have to get out of here. But tomorrow morning we continue this conversation. No arguments! Meet me at sunrise at the Visitor Center at the bluff. You don't have anything else to do, and I'm guessing that you might not be sleeping all that well anyway. We don't have morning Mass on Saturday. So, I get up early, park my car at the Visitor Center, hike to the top, and watch the sun come up. It's glorious and we can continue this. So, get your rear end in that flashy Porsche and meet me there. Okay? Promise me."

He sounds like my drill sergeant in basic training. He doesn't wait for an answer.

"Okay, good. See you in the morning."

# 13

The time with Billy has dragged into late afternoon. The sun is moving lower in the sky. Nightfall is still an hour or so away. A slight headache is beginning its troublesome advent on the top of my head. It feels like some big claw has clamped on to it and is slowly getting tighter. These headaches are becoming more frequent, probably a reaction to the endless stress in my life.

Grandma's car is not in the driveway when I get back to her house. A note on the kitchen counter tells me I probably won't see her until sometime tomorrow.

*Charlie…out for the evening with some friends. Make yourself at home. Help yourself to whatever you can find in the refrigerator. If I don't see you tonight, I will catch up with you tomorrow.*

Food is the last thing on my mind. My appetite is nonexistent. I need to sit down and think about what Billy had to say. Making my way out the back door, I know Grandpa's cabin will give me some space to grapple with this decision I need to make, and more importantly, how I'm going to tell Nora.

Billy's words about God are troubling. If God is real, then I have no idea where he is or what he might be doing. He seems to have a strange habit of staying out of the way. If God is up there, he's not saying much.

Life right now is a huge blur. Everything seems gray and lifeless. As the evening begins to push away the waning daylight, the dark, suffocating edges around my life seem to be getting larger and much closer.

And freedom! What is that? What does that look like? What does that feel like?

Those questions take me back to that summer after we met. Before I started my summer job at a small coffee shop in Kansas City, I decided to take a long-distance bike ride to Wisconsin to see Nora and meet her parents. So, I hopped on my motorcycle and headed north. Five hundred miles and about ten hours later, I drove into the Sullivan dairy farm west of Marshfield.

The image of that moment is still seared into my memory. The picturesque beauty of the farm was something you might see on a postcard. A smattering of fluffy white cumulus clouds dotted the deep blue sky. The big red barn with its large grain silos stood off to the left of the large, white farmhouse. Several dozen Holstein cows with their distinctive black and white markings were moseying out of the barn. What turned out to be their late afternoon milking had just finished.

Nora followed right behind. She was wearing a light blue denim work shirt and jeans. Her hair was pulled back, a red bandana keeping it in place and tied in a knot on the back of her neck. She didn't have much makeup on, but her cheeks were flushed from the work. She didn't see me right away, but as I watched her wipe her brow and take a deep breath, I knew this lady was incredible. I think it was then I realized, maybe for the first time, that I might be falling in love with her. When she finally realized I was there, she ran and jumped into my arms.

"Oh, Charlie, what a surprise! I know it's only been a few weeks since we've seen each other, but somehow it feels like months. I've missed you so much."

We kissed and held each other for a few moments. Only a few of the dairy cows were watching. I had missed her, too.

Her parents were great. We hit it off right away. Call them Jim and Cathy, they said. I could tell quickly their Catholic faith was an important part of their lives. A crucifix was hanging in the living room and a statue of the Holy Family sat on top of the piano in the family room. Their big family dinners with Nora, her two brothers, and two sisters started with a prayer.

The reverent, quiet "Amen" quickly changed into a succession of rapid pass-the-meat-how-about-some-potatoes-what's-for-dessert commands. The raucous noise of the family dinner was startling. Everyone had something to say, and no one minded saying it loudly. It was here that I was introduced to that Wisconsin delicacy called cheese curds. Nora's two brothers even encouraged me to help milk the cows. I begged off saying I was a "city boy" and a slow learner. That began what seemed to be nonstop bantering about how someone like me, a bloke from Nebraska and a student in pre-law, really wasn't smart enough to be around cows. We laughed a lot. For those few days I was there, I felt very much at home.

I remember, too, the day trip Nora and I took to Rib Mountain State Park. It took me awhile to convince her parents that I would take good care of their daughter and I knew what I was doing on my Honda Gold Wing touring bike. My dad was a big motorcycle enthusiast and taught me how to ride. He helped me buy the bike near the end of my junior year in high school. We spent most weekends on the roads of western Nebraska, eastern Wyoming, and northern Colorado. I had a lot of miles under my all-weather riding jeans. The only mishap was sliding into the rear end of Nora's car.

With some reluctance, her dad and mom gave their okay. After the morning milking, Nora and I hopped on the bike and headed east into the farmlands of central Wisconsin. Maybe that was a taste of the freedom Billy was talking about.

It was a glorious morning. Under a bright blue sky, the temperature hovered around the mid-sixties. Having Nora on the bike was one of those special moments. The rush of air blasting our faces and blowing through our hair heightened our senses as we explored the countryside. Nora had her arms around my waist. As we picked up speed, I could feel her grip grow tighter. When we slowed down, her arms relaxed. Her head was nestled comfortably against my back to help block the persistent wind. There was a oneness, a closeness, that made me feel like we were part of a moment that could genuinely be called perfect.

About three miles from the state park, a morning rainstorm suddenly popped up out of nowhere. By the time we made it into the park and found shelter in a picnic area, the two of us were drenched. Two little wet puppies laughing and laughing at the predicament we now faced. I remember how we sat on a picnic table, holding each other close and shivering in the gentle breeze that blew through the park. The rain had not dampened our day. I remember holding Nora close and gently kissing the raindrops off her hair and forehead. It only made the day even more perfect. I could only stay a few days with Nora and her family, but the time in Wisconsin helped me know clearly this was the woman I wanted to spend the rest of my life with.

Today everything has changed. That time with Nora in Wisconsin is only a memory that is getting crammed down into a sea of darkness. It's time to look at that chapter of our lives and stamp it with "The End." It's time to move on.

Grandpa's cabin is quiet. His library of books lined up across the wall of shelves is intimidating. I wonder if he had time to read all of these books. The crucifixes, the statues, and the framed quotes all stand silently, like they are staring at me and calling out to me. I can almost hear the books say, "Read me. You can find some answers here."

Yeah, like books can talk or speak any words to me! I don't think so! As my eyes slowly move across the shelves, I notice a small blue frame sitting on a stack of three books on one of the top shelves. I get up from the chair, move closer, and gently grab the frame.

> **"WHEN YOU ARE GOING THROUGH SOMETHING HARD**
> **AND WONDER WHERE GOD IS REMEMBER –**
> **THE TEACHER IS ALWAYS SILENT DURING THE TEST."**

If this is a test, the silence is earsplitting. If God is real, then he's pretty damn quiet right now.

Taking a deep breath, I can tell something deep inside is beginning to stir. If I'm honest, it feels like my heart is beginning to break. Tears begin to fill my eyes. All of those wonderful times with Nora are so real. But the deep, pressing pain now haunting our life and our marriage is equally real.

As I put the tiny frame back in its place, I again see my grandpa's journal. Part of me knows that reading more of it might be a pseudo-violation of this man's deepest thoughts. Something like a real-life confession, which I'm not sure I should read or have the right to read. As I rationalize that reading another page won't hurt anyone and who would know anyway, I reach for the journal and pull it off the shelf.

*What's the use? What's the purpose? If death is the ultimate end, then what are we are doing and why are we doing it?*

*It seems almost like a gigantic waste of time to simply while away our existence. Day after day, moment by moment, waiting for a moment that could be a mere day away or maybe ten thousand days away. Waiting! Waiting for that single moment when it's all over.*

*What's the use? What's the purpose? If any of this thing called life makes sense, the only way that can begin to happen is to recognize and accept that there might be some higher power that created everything. A Creator! God! Some big, commanding hand somewhere who put a finger on all the world has to offer. Everything! And everyone, including me.*

*But if God is real, where is he? Where are you, God? Why can't I see you? Why can't I hear you? Why can't I touch you? I wonder if I can't see God, or hear him, or touch him, does that mean he is not real?*

*I know during the night I can't see the sun. Does that mean the sun does not exist? Under a blanket of nighttime clouds, I can't see the moon or the stars. Does that mean the moon and the stars don't exist?*

*Because I can't see the snow-covered Alps in Switzerland, or the swarms of fish swimming through the coral reefs of some island in the South Pacific, or the herds of wildebeest migrating through the Serengeti, or a colony of penguins waddling across the ice of Antarctica doesn't mean they don't exist.*

*I can't hear the roar of the waves exploding on a distant seashore or troops of monkeys howling in the Amazon rain forest. Does that mean they don't exist? How could I possibly believe any of that is not real or doesn't exist?*

*So, maybe I can't see God or hear him or touch him, but maybe that doesn't mean he is not real and doesn't exist.*

*Maybe!*

Tears are now filling my eyes. I wonder. Could Billy be right? Could God really be who he says he is? I thought God was a God of mercy and love. Then where are you, God? Where is your mercy? Where is your love?

Wiping the moisture from my eyes, I find myself questioning if perhaps I don't have the eyes to see him. Maybe, I wonder, could I not have the heart to know him? Is this all a question of having faith? I used to have faith. I think!

I'm tired. I need some sleep.

# 14

The night was fretful. The hours inched by like a lava flow down the side of an active volcano. The cauldron of hot fire inside me boiled and bubbled all night. Any idea of getting some sleep was a joke. My thoughts of Nora and our marriage became a nightlong wrestling match between figuring out how to tell her what I have to tell her and finalizing this merger deal next week. That morphed into a war of words about God. If he is real, where is he? I know the sun is somewhere on the other side of the planet, grizzly bears are growling in Alaska, and hyenas are laughing somewhere in Africa, but I don't have a clue where God is.

Now as I ease my car into a parking spot at the Visitor Center, sunrise is still a half hour away. I can see the dark shadow of Billy leaning on the only other parked car in the lot. I've never been too crazy about heights. The thought of hiking to the top of a big rock to watch the sun come up and doing that near the edge of a cliff with a drop off of almost three football fields is beginning to turn my stomach. Billy spins his head as he hears me approaching and puts a finger to his lips.

"Be quiet," he whispers.

He starts walking and motions me to follow him.

"Listen!"

It's another soft whisper as he cocks his head like he's listening for some sound off in the distance.

"Listen to what? All I hear is our feet hitting the path. There's nothing to listen to."

"Sure there is. The whole world right now is groaning in the creation of a new day. It's in the silence that we find God. I heard once that silence is the language of God. That's a language we can all understand."

Here we go again. More God talk! I could be sleeping. Or at least, trying to sleep.

"Look, Charlie, you can't see it or maybe hear it, but all of creation is coming to life right in front of us. No word is spoken, but the trees are extending their roots looking for water and nourishment. The prairie grasses are doing the same thing. The wind is rushing across the prairie, then up and over the side of the bluff. That gentle breeze across our faces and everything else we see in front of us is the hand of God creating the gift of a new day for us. But the eyes of your heart would have to let you know that and help you see what is sitting right in front of us this morning."

Billy is quiet again as we continue our hike to the top. The eastern sky is losing some of its dark edges. The morning clouds are beginning to reflect the new-day light as if they are anticipating a glorious sunrise.

"And look at the stars. Their light is beginning to fade away. Do you know how many stars there are? Scientists estimate there are three sextrillion stars in the universe. That would be a three with twenty-three zeroes. We can't even begin to comprehend what that means. It's unfathomable. But that is the nature of God. His love and mercy for you and for me are incomprehensible. But when we sit quietly and marvel at what is called the Book of Nature, we can begin to catch a fleeting glimpse of who God is."

I don't have much to say, and the silence of the morning is starting to feel increasingly uncomfortable. I didn't think Billy could be quiet this long.

"I used to come up here a lot when we were in high school. I spent a lot of Saturday mornings looking out over the plains wondering what God had in mind for me and my life. The call to the priesthood was still rattling around my life a bit. I think I was hoping he had some other plan for me. Anything but the priesthood! I would think then and even think today about something St. Gregory the Great talked about. He would talk about dawn yielding to the day and we end up in a murky, not-quite-complete moment like this one we have right now. We know the night is ending, but we don't yet have the full light of day. St. Gregory points out that all of us trying to find the truth of life are living between the darkness of night and the full light of day. So, we are stuck, so to speak, in this gray area. We don't have all the answers. As I like to say, we aren't sure we even know what the question is. It's in our questions that we discover and recognize that life is a mystery. We know we want more. In our own way we keep seeking the light. We may not be able to articulate it, but all of us are really seeking God, who is the source of that light and life itself. I suspect your life right now is still in the dark of your night. But the light of day is coming, if you give God the permission he needs to lead you to it."

Billy is much too philosophical for this wayward soul.

"But, you know, Charlie, the sunrises teach me a lot about God and his creation. He is ever present. He is always creating and always calling us to more. Some mornings out here it seems like God has two big cans of paint, one black and one gray. Then with a giant brush and a vigorous hand he slaps the black and gray paint across the horizon and turns the sky into a mass of dark, foreboding, low-hanging clouds. Then he adds some deep, rumbling thunder and fills the dark skies with a steady downpour to water and cleanse the earth."

More silence!

"Then there are days like this one is starting to be. I have this image of God standing over us with an enormous art palette. The palette is dotted with a host of different colors. Oranges and yellows. Some reds and blues. A smudge of white on the edge of the palette helps this Master Artist temper and lighten the different shades. I see him using a small brush with a fine tip that he swings through the sky to add an ever-changing flair to his morning masterpiece. It's amazing to watch God's creative hand giving us this gift of a new day."

Billy lets out a big sigh as he seems to be drinking in the expanding beauty of the morning.

"You know, Charlie, I wasn't sure I'd see you here this morning."

"Well, I promised. So, here I am."

Billy slowly turns away from the emerging dawn and looks directly at me.

"Good to know you can keep some of your promises."

"What do you mean by that?"

"My apologies. I could have been a bit kinder with that remark. But I keep thinking about your promise to Nora, the one to love and honor her all the days of your life."

It's still dark enough that Billy probably can't see my face turning to an angry red. Why do I keep agreeing to see this guy?

"You know, Charlie, I find it interesting how married couples talk about their wedding day. They'll say Father So-and-So married us. Or it was our pastor who married us. In the Sacrament of Marriage in the Catholic Church, the priest is only there as a witness to represent the Church. He doesn't marry the couple. It is the man and woman who marry one another. The vows are made to each other.

Those words are part of a covenant, a divine commitment, made by one man and one woman with God. With all due respect, this is not some legal contract where you can put on your fancy lawyer suit with an expensive silk tie, waltz into some court of law, have some judge listen to your dispute, and decide for you or against you."

Billy's frustration is growing.

"On the day of your wedding, you made a covenant with Nora and with God. The words you spoke – no doubt from your heart that day – in front of the priest, your family, and your friends were what you declared to do with this lady you claimed you were going to love for the rest of your life. The words you said were serious. Everyone, and I mean everyone, including God, took you at your word."

Billy looks away and turns toward the sunrise.

"So, Charlie, what do you know about Hiram Scott?"

Oh, good, he's changing the subject.

"Not too much. He was a fur trader. He died somewhere around here. Scotts Bluff is what people called it. It became a landmark on the Oregon Trail."

"That's all true, Charlie. But I wondered one day if there might be more to the story. So, I went back and did some research. The legend of Hiram Scott goes back to around 1826 or 1827. Scott was said to be a clerk for the Rocky Mountain Fur Company. He was effectively the money guy who kept track of the furs during the trading rendez-vous with the native Indians. Early records show he was born in 1805 in St. Charles County, Missouri, a little west of St. Louis. A big man, about six feet four, weighed about 250 pounds and very strong, they say. He was said to be traveling with a party of fur traders apparently on their way back to St. Louis to sell their furs."

Billy turns to face west and points.

"About sixty miles northwest of here, on the upper part of the Platte River, near Fort Laramie, Wyoming, their flimsy bark canoes somehow capsized. Their gunpowder and all their supplies were thrown into the water and ruined. Now they would need to walk out. With no gunpowder, their rifles were effectively useless. They had to rely on the native roots and wild fruits to survive. But somewhere during the journey, Scott was either injured or taken sick. No one knows exactly what happened. Because Scott can't travel, the party decided to leave two of the men with him near Fort Laramie until he gets stronger. But after a few days, those two men decide Scott was not going to make it. So, they left him to chase after and catch up with the main party. Scott was left in this wilderness to essentially fend for himself. It would be a year later that another party would find the skeleton of Scott at the base of the bluff. The story says all they found were bleached bones, but because of the size of the skeleton along with some papers and clothing, they were able to identify the remains as those of Hiram Scott. He was said to have been buried somewhere around here. No one knows exactly where."

"So, if he is so sick or so hurt, how did he get here to the bluff?"

"Well, no one really knows. But somehow Scott managed to crawl or limp across about sixty miles of wilderness to get here. When I think about what he had to do to try to survive, I don't know how he got even this far. I mean, he had to drag himself across sixty miles of Nebraska wilderness, protecting himself from who knows how many wild animals, crossing rivers, navigating the badlands and their nearly impassable steep, rocky slopes. He probably had no food to speak of either. I look over this vast, wide-open expanse and think about his loneliness and fear and doing whatever he had to do to find help and live through the ordeal. I wonder, too, at times how he died. No food, I'm sure. Maybe some water he could find in the Platte. But all alone. No one anywhere close by. He had been abandoned by the only people he knew and he was left alone to die."

Billy is silent again. He's looking out over the plains and watching the morning sky grow brighter. He slowly turns his head toward me. His eyes, as if they are looking into the depths of my soul, are riveted on mine.

"You know, Charlie, as I think about the story of Hiram Scott and how he was abandoned by his friends, I would say to you that that's exactly what you are about to do to Nora and your children. With all due respect, if you walk away from your marriage, you will be abandoning your wife and family to fend for themselves. They will be desperately alone. No doubt they will be hurt and angry and have no idea what to do or how to go on without you. I have seen enough families go through times like these to know that you will devastate Nora and destroy your family."

My breath has been sucked out of me. Billy's words are a gut-punch unlike any I have ever experienced. I can't believe he would say something like that. My response is slow and deliberate.

"Well, Billy, let me say this! With all due respect, screw you!"

# 15

Steering my car back down Grandma's gravel driveway, I see a single light in her family room. She's probably praying. Talking with her right now is not something I want to do. So, I pull back to Grandpa's cabin. Once inside I plop down in the leather chair. I am tired. Physically and emotionally. I feel drained. Empty and confused.

I hardly remember the hike down from the bluff or the twenty-minute drive back to Grandma's. My hands clenched the steering wheel as if I were strangling it. Maybe that's what I wanted to do to Billy. I'm not sure what I expected talking with him would do, but I sure didn't expect to hear those kinds of insults.

Abandoning Nora? Come on, Billy! You don't think that I'd be sure she would be taken care of? You don't think I'd make sure the kids would be okay? Of course I would! Once this deal is completed, there will be plenty of money for everyone. They'll be fine.

I am suddenly aware that my jaw hurts. Clenched teeth probably don't help. My thoughts are racing and my breathing is slow and measured. The anger seems to be pouring through me like an unrelenting mountain waterfall. I thought priests were supposed to be charitable.

As my eyes turn to Grandpa's library of books, I push myself out of the chair to look more closely at the titles. Maybe some words of wisdom can be found on some page in one of these. Who are you people who think you have any sort of insight into the heartaches of life? Who are you that you think you are so wise that someone would want to read what you have to say? And it's a sure bet there is nothing on these shelves written by Fr. Billy Donahue. Who does he think he is?

What makes you people think you know so much about God? Who are you, John Henry Newman? And who are you, Josef Pieper? And Hilaire Belloc, who are you? Ronald Knox, what about you? I've never heard anything about any of you. The burning anger is fueling my sarcasm.

And here's a name I can't even pronounce. Jean-Pierre de Caussade. As I pull that book off the shelf, I'm struck by its title. *Abandonment to Divine Providence.* I go from being accused of abandoning my wife to a book about abandonment. So, Jean-Pierre, what do you know about abandonment?

A bookmark is sticking out of the top. What words of wisdom do you have, Jean Pierre? Sitting back down in Grandpa's big chair, I push the bookmark aside. I wonder what this holy know-it-all has to say about whatever he thinks he's talking about.

*I*t is true that a canvas simply and blindly offered to the brush feels at each moment only the stroke of the brush. It is the same with a lump of stone. Each blow from the hammering of the sculptor's chisel makes it feel – if it could – as if it were being destroyed.

*As blow after blow descends, the stone knows nothing of how the sculptor is shaping it. All it feels is a chisel chopping away at it, cutting it, and mutilating it. For example, let's take a piece of stone destined to be carved into a crucifix or a statue.*

*We might ask it: "What do you think is happening to you?" And it might answer: "Don't ask me. All I know is that I must stay immovable in the hands of the sculptor, and I must love him and endure all he inflicts on me to produce the figure he has in mind. He knows how to do it."*

*As for me, I have no idea what he is doing, nor do I know what he will make of me. But what I do know is that his work is the best possible. It is perfect.*

*I welcome each blow of the chisel as the best thing that could happen to me, although, if I'm to be truthful, I feel that every one of these blows is ruining me, destroying me, and disfiguring me. But I remain unconcerned. I concentrate on the present moment, think only of my duty, and suffer all that this master sculptor inflicts on me without knowing his purpose or fretting about it.*

I can hardly breathe. It's like whatever his name is, Jean-Pierre de Caussade, knows exactly what I'm going through. Right now every heartbeat feels like some hammer and chisel knocking fault lines in the center of my chest. With each blow my entire life feels like it's being ruined, destroyed, and disfigured. Yes, that is absolutely what is happening. I can feel it in the depths of my soul.

But hammer away, God! Your big chisel is chipping away at everything I've ever known. Your hammer is brutal. It's like a jackhammer that is heavy, merciless, and smashing me to my knees. I find myself sneering under my breath, "If you're real, God, stop it! Stop it!"

My heart is heavy. Emotionally I am spent. Tears again well up in my eyes. As I glance back at the books, my eyes slowly make their way back to Grandpa's journal.

"I don't know, Grandpa," I mutter to myself. "Do I dare check out one more entry? So personal, so private, but so real. Would you have any more insights for me? Would you care if I read one more?"

One more, I think to myself. Just one more! Getting up from the chair and moving toward the books, I reach for the journal and cautiously pull it off the shelf. My words are virtually inaudible, "So, what have you got to say for yourself?"

*I am beginning to understand that every decision in life has a* consequence. It can be good. It can be bad. But every choice I make will have an outcome. Something will happen. Good or bad, something will happen.

The world is telling me that power and money and fame will lead me to the happiness I am searching for. But more and more it seems those promises are sick and empty. They all seem to be leading to a life of unhappiness. It's like life is being built on a stunning fear of failure.

If I don't achieve what the world tells me I should be seeking, then my life will have been for naught. If I don't make a certain amount of money or drive a certain kind of car or live in a certain kind of house, then life is nothing but a colossal failure. It's a lonely kind of existence. And the loneliness that fear of failure breeds is staggering.

I have this image that I am standing on the side of a small mountain lake. The air is crisp and cool. The breeze is a gentle one. A few wispy clouds are floating across a remarkably blue sky.

I'm holding a small stone in each hand. The stones are about the size of a half dollar. On one is written "Quit" and on the other is "Don't Quit." In this imaginary game, of sorts, the rules say that I can only throw one stone into the lake. So, I have to choose which one. "Quit" or "Don't Quit." But whatever choice I make, when that stone hits the clear, calm lake, it will create a series of ripples. Those small waves will cascade away from the splash, and for the time being, one tiny part of this body of water will change.

It's the same in life. Every choice impacts the life of someone else. Our choices, good or bad, ripple out into the lives of the people we know and probably even some we don't know. Think about that car accident on some big city freeway that is blocking all lanes of traffic and now hundreds and hundreds of cars are stopped dead on the highway. All because of an accident they had nothing to do with. The ripples from that accident could include making someone late for work and an important presentation; another person is going to miss the big job interview; someone else is trying to get to a hospital to see a dying relative; so many lives impacted by a choice they had nothing to do with. So, when we make a choice, that decision will create ripples in the lives of others and, whether we like it or not, will impact their lives in one way or another.

In the game of life a lot of times the easiest thing to do is give up and toss the "Quit" stone into the water. The reality of that choice is it's easy because it's all about me. It's wrapped up in what I want to do and what I think is good and best for me. The truth is that I don't care how those currents touch the lives of anyone else. I don't care because those consequences don't mean anything to me. In so many ways that choice to quit is heartless and selfish.

Tossing the "Don't Quit" stone into the water is the tougher choice. That would mean someone else might be more important than what I want. That would mean that I might care more about the good of someone else. That might mean that I was thinking of others first and trying to do what was best for them.

In the end, quitting leads to a life of regrets and an ongoing chorus of "what-ifs." What if I had done this? What if I hadn't done that? What if I hadn't quit? What if I had tried one more thing? What if I hadn't given up? What if? What if? What if?

So, for today I think the choice is to toss that "Don't Quit" stone into the pond. I don't know how the ripples will ripple out, but I am going to trust in the good choice and what I hope is the better choice. Because it seems to me that good will always build on good.

But what about that "Quit" stone? Let's bury that one somewhere in a deep, dark crater. I'll remember where it is. Because I can always dig it up and quit. That's the easy thing to do. For now I will save quitting for another day.

Replacing the journal back in the bookcase, I can only lament that it's all too late. It feels like I've already tossed my "Quit" stone into the air. It seems as if it is now flipping in slow motion toward splashdown on the surface of the lake. Easing myself back into Grandpa's chair, I keep telling myself Nora and the kids will be okay. They don't need me. But now I'm beginning to have some doubts. I'm not so sure.

# 16

I must have fallen asleep in Grandpa's big chair, because the next thing I know Grandma is gently touching my shoulder.

"Charlie! Hey, Charlie, I'm sorry to wake you."

I feel like I've been pulled out of a deep sleep. It takes me a few seconds to remember where I am and what I'm doing here.

"Hi, Grandma. Wow, I must have really been tired. What's going on?"

"You have a visitor. He says you probably don't want to talk to him, but Fr. Bill is here."

Well, that's the understatement of the decade. Billy is the last person I expected to see today and certainly the last person I want to talk with right now.

"What does he want?"

"He said he just wanted to talk. Something about your conversation this morning not ending too well. And he was looking to see how you're doing."

"Tell him I'm resting and now is not a good time."

"You tell him. He's right outside."

Grandma turns to leave, opens the door, and says, "Fr. Bill, he's right here. He says he really wants to talk with you."

Billy walks slowly through the open door as Grandma heads back to the main house. He makes his way to the fireplace and sits down on the hearth. His look is surly and serious.

"I'm not here to apologize. But our conversation wasn't over."

"Well, it was sure over for me. What an insulting thing to say! Abandoning my wife and children? Where do you get off making that kind of accusation?"

"What do you call it? If it's not abandonment, what is it?"

The air is thick with a conspicuous uneasiness. We both sit there for what seems to be a few agonizing, edgy minutes.

"Look, Charlie, this is the time when you need to fight for your marriage. I mean literally fight for the future of you and Nora and the kids. It's pretty clear that you are giving up. I'm here to tell you that you don't have to do that. I'm confident that if you go through with what you think you have to do, you will live a life full of regrets. You'll wonder for the rest of your life if you really did the right thing. You don't want to do this. Give it a chance. Give this some time. Come back to the Church and let God back into your life. I'll be in church this afternoon. Come back to confession, get back in the good graces of God, and let's begin to put your marriage back on some solid ground. In fact, you know what? If you want, I can hear your confession right now, right here."

"Look, Billy, I checked and confession is simply not on my list of things to do today. It's a waste of time. It doesn't change anything. Telling a priest about all of the crud in my life doesn't do anyone any good at all."

"With all due respect, I would say that's just your pride and ego talking. You're telling me that Charlie is too good, too perfect, too okay just the way he is to be bothered with some way to find peace and a sense of hope in his life. Always need to be right, don't you? You just can't admit you might be wrong about the way you act and might need to be forgiven by God and the people you might have hurt in some way. Right?"

Billy needs to shut up. I don't need any of this religious crap.

"And tell me, Billy, why would I have to go to a priest anyway? I can just go straight to God."

"You can do that, but then you don't hear the actual words of absolution. You simply 'think' you've been forgiven. When we hear the priest tell us that we have been absolved from our sins, it's different. The burdens, the pain, the sins can literally be lifted from us. We can in every sense of the word be healed."

"And then I just go out and sin again, don't I?"

"Yes, you do. We all do. That's how it works. And that's why this Sacrament of Confession can be so life-giving. Because we do sin again. But we can go back and tell God again how we have fallen, how we have come up short, and how we want to begin again."

"I don't think so, Billy. Not going to happen! Confession is for losers."

"This is all very, very obvious, Charlie. Right now you're slowly sinking into some watery abyss. I would bet that you might be having some doubts about ending your marriage. But I can see the water is up to your chin and you're about to drown. This isn't good, Charlie. You don't have to quit. Divorce is not the answer."

What does he know? I haven't seen this dude-turned-priest for almost two decades, and in less than two days, he thinks he knows what this life is like. Give me a great big damn break!

"See, Billy, you just don't get it. I'm not sure what's happened to us, but it's not good. In fact, I ask myself all of the time what happened to us. And I don't have an answer for that question."

97

"It's a good question, Charlie. But I think you're asking the wrong question. I would venture this is not a matter of what happened to the two of you. The real question is what happened to you."

"What do you mean what happened to me? I'm not the one who doesn't want to make love. I'm not the one who doesn't seem to have any time to do the things we used to do. I'm not the one who wants to stay home on weekends."

Billy is looking at me again with that glare of disapproval.

"No, you're the one who wants to work on weekends and leave a tired wife at home with the kids. You're not the one spending every day of the week with two demanding children. And you're not the one feeling used in your sexual relationship. Why do you think she would want to do anything with you? It's like you don't care about her or what she's dealing with and what might be best for her. But Charlie, let's be very clear. Nora hasn't changed your marriage. You have! As I listen to you, it's all about you and what you want. When was the last time you thought about Nora first and listened to her and treated her like she deserves to be treated?"

Billy is losing his patience and getting angrier by the minute. His voice is agitated and snarly.

"So, yes, your marriage has changed. But you need to look at your-self and figure out the role you've played in that. Don't blame Nora for all that's happened."

In his exasperation, he lets out a sigh and leans back against the fireplace.

"Come on, Charlie, don't quit without giving it a chance. I said it before and I'll say it again. If you want things to change in your mar-riage, Charlie has to change Charlie first. But ditching your marriage commitment without fighting for it is the coward's way out."

Coward! Does he have any idea what courage this is taking?

"Look, Charlie, Nora didn't sign up for this. She would never have dreamed sixteen years ago that the man she vowed to spend the rest of her life with would one day say goodbye and walk out the door."

I hear all of that, but we are way past the point of no return. It's over and I don't understand why he doesn't get it.

"So, Billy, you 're probably thinking I'm a jerk, aren't you?"

"It's crossed my mind."

"I get a lot of that these days."

"Yeah, I bet you do."

We are now glowering at one another. Our eyes are locked in some sort of staring contest waiting for the other one to blink. Billy loses and blinks first.

"So, Charlie, do you remember the baseball game in the state play-offs against North Platte High? It was my senior year. You were a junior. We were down five runs in the last inning. Do you remember that?"

"Yeah, I do. That was some game, wasn't it?"

"Of all the games I've played, high school and college, that's the game I never forget. So, it's the last inning, we're down by five runs, and we have two outs. Coach comes over to the dugout, looks all of us in the eye, and points his finger at each one of us. 'No one quits,' he says. 'We don't need five runs. We need one hit. And then we need another one. And another one. Just get your hit. The runs will take care of themselves.' And that's what happened. It started. One hit. Then another. And another. You got one. I got one. And Coach was right. We got six runs and at the end of the inning we were up by one. Pretty amazing comeback, for sure."

I remember that game like it was yesterday. I also remember we lost.

"But don't forget, Billy. We lost. They got two runs in their bottom half of the inning and we were out of the playoffs."

"That's right. Do you remember how we lost?"

"I'm not sure. Mostly I remember the comeback."

"Well, I lost the game for us. There were two outs. One more out and we win the game. They have runners on first and third, and a line drive single comes to me in right field. The runner on third scores and ties the game. The runner on first is sprinting to third base. I field the ball and then airmail it about ten feet over the third baseman's head. The runner scores and they win the game. Remember it now?"

"Yeah, I do. You did lose it for us, didn't you?"

"I sure did. But think about this, Charlie! You remember the comeback. I remember the error. The point is that we didn't give up. Sure, we lost, but we didn't give up on each other as a team. We stayed with it and look at what happened. So, come on, Charlie! I don't want you to give up on your marriage. Don't give up on each other. I've never met Nora, and I am confident she has her quirks and she does things that drive you nuts. But be honest! You have your quirks and you do things that drive her nuts. It's called life. It's what happens in marriages. You're not alone in what you're going through. Trust me, every married couple goes through these tough times. A lot of couples aren't honest about it, but every marriage has its rough moments. The issue then is what are you going to do about it."

"I don't know, Billy. I just don't think it can work anymore."

"Coach told us to focus on getting just one hit at a time. Look at what happened. I'm asking you to stay with this. Take it one day at a time. Don't worry about the next ten or twenty years of your life. Deal with this day. Just today. Right now. This moment. Then tomorrow you can deal with tomorrow. The day after that you can deal with that day."

"But we will just be putting off the inevitable. If this divorce is eventually going to happen one day down the road, then why put it off? Let's get it over with."

"I'm going to presume you already have the divorce papers ready to file. They're probably in your briefcase and you're trying to figure out how to gently tell Nora you want to split. Right?"

He's right. The papers are ready. I only have to give them to Nora.

"That's correct. They're in a file folder in my briefcase. All she has to do is sign them."

"So, here is my suggestion. Give your life with Nora a chance. Go back home and put that file folder in a drawer in your desk at the office. But try to make your life with Nora work first. I mean, you work like a madman to put this merger deal together and build your business. Well, work just that hard to build up and revitalize your marriage and your life with Nora and the kids. Do that first, knowing that file folder with the divorce papers is sitting in that desk drawer. You can always pull it out."

"I don't know, Billy. I see no hope in any of this. It's so clear that this marriage is over. I think we need to accept that. I think *you* need to accept that. It's time to move on."

# 17

"Tell me about your wedding day. What do you remember about it?"

Man, he just doesn't give up, does he? I find myself shaking my head at the question.

"It was a nice day. We got married. As I think back on it, not much to it."

"You know what, Charlie? That's pathetic. What do you mean there wasn't much to it?"

Our staring contest continues. I can tell he's frustrated. Which is good! Maybe he'll get out of here and leave me alone.

"I know you don't want to talk about this. And that's too bad. Humor me. I really want to know what you remember. That specific day was the day you began to build your life together. It should have been a day full of hope and promise. It should have been a glorious day. And it probably was."

My thoughts are scrambling back in time trying to resurrect some memory of our wedding day. I'm having trouble. The anger in both of us is becoming more intense. This time I lose the staring contest.

I look away as I begin to recall that day in June almost sixteen years ago.

"So, next month it's sixteen years. See I remember! Does that make you happy?"

"Yeah, I'm happy. Now tell me about your wedding day. What was the weather like? June in Wisconsin has to be a nice time of the year, right?"

"It was a nice day. The church, St. John the Baptist, sits across from a rather delightful city park. It was a bit overcast, but the temperature was pleasant and the humidity was low. I remember waiting with all of the groomsmen in the sacristy. I could hear friends and family outside making their way inside the church. I was nervous, but anxious to get going. I couldn't wait to see Nora. I do remember that!"

"What was the church like?"

"It was long and narrow. It seemed like it took close-to-forever for the bridesmaids and Nora to walk down the aisle. I do remember on either side of the altar there were these high wooden altars. The wood was dark. Statues of Jesus, Mary, St. Joseph, and a few others really made it all quite impressive.

"And Nora? She must have looked beautiful."

My anger is beginning to cool down. The memory of her walking down the aisle is as vivid and real as if it were happening again in this very moment.

"Yeah, she was gorgeous. I could tell she was nervous. She clutched her father's arm like she never wanted to let go. But her eyes were sparkling and excited. Her smile was charming and honestly irresistible. I remember thinking that this beautiful lady was about to become my wife. I felt so proud that I was about to be her husband. The closeness I felt to her at that moment was remarkable."

Billy is listening closely. He lets me sit with the memory for a moment. His slight smile tells me he's enjoying the memory of that day, too.

"Do you remember your priest asking you some questions?"

"What do you mean? Like what?"

"He asked you and Nora three of them. Have you come here to enter into marriage without coercion, freely and wholeheartedly? Are you prepared, as you follow the path of marriage, to love and honor each other for as long as you both shall live? Are you prepared to accept children lovingly from God and to bring them up according to the law of Christ and his Church?"

"Okay, I do remember that."

"And I will presume you answered 'yes' to all of those questions. You, Nora, and everyone there believed that you were there freely, that you would love and honor each other for as long as you live, and that you would be open to having children as God so willed it. Right?"

"That's right."

"So, you were there freely, but you maybe weren't so sure about loving each other for as long as you live and having children. Well, Charlie, forgive me, but one out of three may be good in baseball, but it's not so good when it comes to love and marriage."

I'm shaking my head again in disbelief that this conversation keeps heading down some dark hole.

"The vows? Do you remember those?"

"Sure! The good times, the bad times, and all of that. I do remember facing each other, looking into one another's eyes, holding hands as we said our vows. How we would squeeze our hands to add some emphasis or meaning to what we were saying."

"And the part of the vows where you promised to love and honor each other for all the days of your life, do you remember that?"

"I do remember that."

"And I presume you didn't have your fingers crossed, right? And you know, don't you, that all the days of your life might be longer than sixteen years?"

"Come on, Billy! Yes, I know that, but things change. We're not the same."

The anger is beginning to boil up again.

"Do you know, Billy, as a priest you are really annoying?"

"It's part of my job description. But to my point earlier, I am only trying to help you not give up. What you had that day of your wedding can be yours again. But you're going to have to work at it. The question is whether you think it's worth it. I happen to think it is worth it. My prayer is that you think it's worth it, too, and are willing to put in a little work to begin healing your marriage."

"I don't know, Billy. I don't see much hope in any of this."

"With all due respect, I would say to you that if you can't find much hope right now, it's because you have pushed God aside and won't let him be part of your marriage."

"Okay, then where is he?"

"Well, he's everywhere. It's pretty clear you don't have the eyes to see that right now, but God is right here right now. But you have to invite him back into your life. You have effectively shoved him out of the way, and he will stay there until you ask him back. It's your choice."

Well, my choice is for Billy to stand up and get out of here. But he's not moving.

"You know, Charlie, everyone gets love mixed up with all of those feel-good emotions. Most of us get it all wrong. Love is choosing what is best for the people in your life. Not what you think is best for you. When you and Nora were first dating, life and love for one another was probably easy. You had good times. You went fun places. The closeness was immeasurable. But love is more than that. A lot more! Love is choosing to walk through the tough times together. Love is climbing the steep mountains of your life together. Love is pushing away what you want to do and doing the right thing for that other person. That doesn't mean you always *like* the other person, but you *choose* to love her. That, Charlie, is what love is all about."

The staring contest resumes.

"I know I wasn't there on your wedding day. But let me see if I can paint the picture of what was going on. So, Nora looks beautiful. You're standing there in your tuxedo and shiny shoes. The bridesmaids look stunning in their matching dresses. Your groomsmen are in their tuxes with colorful cummerbunds to match yours. All of your family and friends are dressed to the nines. Everyone is smiling and eager to be part of this incredible day when you become Mr. and Mrs. Charles Landis. Is that a fair description?"

"Yeah, that's pretty good actually."

"So, in the middle of this once-in-a-lifetime celebration where you and Nora are going to promise yourselves to one another for the rest of your lives, one thing sort of goes unnoticed. Any idea what that might be?"

"I don't know. What?"

"Well, above the altar in the middle of everything that's going on, a dead guy is hanging on a tree. What's that all about?"

Billy is quiet. He is obviously waiting for an answer I don't have.

"Well, Charlie, that is exactly what it is all about! Jesus Christ loved all of us so much that he gave his life for us. Jesus loves you and Nora so much that he gave his life for the two of you. Jesus sacrificed himself so that all of us might have life. Jesus is telling us and telling you that your life with Nora is all about sacrifice. On your wedding day you were called to give your life for her. You promised you would do that. You were called to die for her every day of your life whether you feel like it or not. It's all about the bride. Jesus died for his Bride, the Church. And when you married Nora, you were called to give your life for Nora, your bride."

Billy is silent again. Hoping, I am sure, that his words might be sinking in.

"The cross for Jesus brought his love to completion. When you, Charlie, make sacrifices for Nora, you bring your love for her to completion. People around you should be able to see the way God loves them by the way you and Nora love one another. When the two of you walk down a street, for instance, and you're holding hands, that's an image of the way God walks with all of us. He walks with all of us when life is good and even when life is a mess. So, when you are faithful to one another in every moment of your life, then we get a glimpse of God's love and fidelity to us. A lot of people are counting on you to be faithful to the promises you made to one another on your wedding day."

Billy looks away, apparently distracted by another thought.

"I think back to my call to the priesthood. I think the final thing for me was realizing the depth of Jesus' love. He loved me, loved all of us so much that he would choose to die. He would sacrifice his own life to be sure all of us had a chance at heaven. In that one act of silent, heroic courage, Jesus would take on my sins, all of our sins as the final sacrifice to God, the Father. That image of Jesus hanging on the cross and dying there for my sins touched me deeply."

"Heroic courage?"

"That's right, Charlie. You know, when we look at the crucifixes in our churches, most of them are fairly tame in terms of what they show us. The truth is at His crucifixion, Jesus is a bloody mess of a man gasping for air. A crown of one-inch-long thorns has been smashed onto his head. Blood is pouring into his eyes and down his face. Six-inch nails have been pounded through his wrists. His arms are outstretched. He can't breathe. His legs are painfully lifting himself up to suck in any breath of air he could in order to stay alive. The deep scourge marks from the brutal whipping have shredded his back. His skin is hanging off his body in strips. The dreadful wounds covered his entire front and back. Then after he was dead, a centurion thrusts a spear into his side with blood and water gushing out. Jesus gave everything for all of us. His last drop of blood was poured out on Calvary, that hill of execution outside the walls of the Old City of Jerusalem two-thousand years ago. He did that for you, for Nora, for me, for everyone. When I realized the love of Jesus was that great, I was overwhelmed and knew I had to say 'yes' to this call to be one of his priests."

Billy's voice is soft and reflective. His eyes are moist as he is reliving the memory.

"One of my favorite letters in Scripture is the one Paul wrote to the Ephesians. The fifth chapter, and I know you know this one, is where Paul says that wives should be subordinate to their husbands. Every time this is read during a Sunday Mass, I watch the men sitting in the congregation. I can see you husbands smiling a bit and sometimes gently putting an elbow into the sides of your wives. You know that verse, don't you?"

I nod my head. For someone who is sometimes biblically illiterate, I do know that one.

"Well, Charlie, what I tell husbands about this passage and what I would say to you is this – keep reading. Paul goes on to say, 'Husbands, love your wives, even as Christ loved the church and handed himself over for her.' He also says that husbands should love their wives as their own bodies. It's all about love and a husband, like you, Charlie, is called to love your wife so much that you would die for her. That means in a time like this, when things are not going well for the two of you, you need to make it all about Nora, not about Charlie and what Charlie believes is best for Charlie."

The stillness in the cabin is unsettling. Billy breaks the silence.

"You keep talking about this merger deal with this other firm in California. But here's the deal, Charlie. On your wedding day you promised Nora that you would be faithful to her in good times and in bad, in sickness and in health, to love and honor her all the days of your life. That's the deal. Not this merger deal you're trying to pull together. Everything you are going through right now, all of this muck and anger and fear, is all part of the real deal. When the two of you made those vows to one another, you gave your word. You made a promise to one another. You did all of that in front of your family and friends and God. You said that you would be faithful to those vows. That's the deal, Charlie. Marriage is for the rest of your lives, not when you get tired and want to quit."

I am getting sick to my stomach. Billy looks sad and genuinely disappointed.

"I know, Billy. I know. I never expected any of this to be part of my life with Nora. But life happens and things change."

"But did you think your life with Nora was going to be easy? Did you think that you would sail through everything without challenges or setbacks? I told you yesterday that your vows talk about the 'bad times.' That's not because bad times *might* happen. That's because bad times *do* happen. That's all part of the deal, Charlie."

"I hear all of this, Billy. I guess I just don't know what to do about it."

"Well, you go home, tell your wife that you love her, and you want to work this out. That's what you do. After you go to confession, come back to church, and invite God back into your life."

I am looking at the floor shaking my head. I again have no words.

"Look, I've got to get going," Billy says with a big sigh. "Like I said, every Saturday afternoon at 3:00 I spend an hour in church praying before the Blessed Sacrament. I hear confessions beginning at 4:00. Mass starts at 5:00. I will be praying for you and Nora and that you find the courage and the strength to get this marriage of yours back on the right track. You have to decide. It's really all up to you."

We make our way toward the cabin door and head outside. I don't have anything to say as we walk back up the driveway. We shake hands and Billy gives me a hug. But my heart's not in it as I turn and walk away.

"I'll be waiting, Charlie."

His tone is encouraging and hopeful. But I mutter to myself, "Don't hold your breath."

# 18

As Billy's car heads down the gravel driveway, Grandma is waiting for me in the kitchen. She is pouring coffee into two mugs, obviously expecting me to sit and talk. Not exactly how I wanted to spend the rest of my morning.

"That didn't look like two old high school buddies saying good-bye after having an enjoyable time together."

"No! I don't think I'd call it 'enjoyable.'"

"Here, sit with me."

I can't believe she wants to talk about this. She settles into her chair and takes a sip of her coffee.

"So, Charlie, what's going on?"

I'm sure the perplexed look on my face tells her I don't want to talk about "what's going on."

"It's Nora, right? You said Thursday night that things weren't so good with the two of you. How serious is this? You aren't thinking about divorcing her, are you?"

Fear begins to well up in my chest. It's one thing to talk with a priest about this, but right now my grandmother doesn't seem to be the right person to share the story of our fragile and fractured marriage. I sip some coffee to gather my thoughts.

"I don't know what to say, Grandma. But we are pretty far down the road to think we have any chance to make things better."

She's not saying anything. Her serious, firm gaze tells me she expects me to carry the weight of the conversation.

"It was good to talk with Billy. Fr. Bill, I mean. He gave me a lot of things to think about. But so many things have changed in our marriage. I think Nora and I both would agree what we have today is not what we thought it would be. Nora does her thing. I do mine. We don't seem to have a lot in common anymore. Our fights are more frequent. It's just not very good."

"Does Nora want this to end?"

"Probably not. But I don't think either of us wants to live the rest of our lives like this."

"What about the kids? Do Robbie and Julie know their dad and mom are considering a divorce and their dad might be walking out?"

"No. And I do worry a little about the impact a divorce will have on them. But they'll be okay. I'm making plenty of money to take care of them and give them everything they will need or want. And Nora, too!"

"I hope you know, Charlie, they won't be okay. What they want and need is a dad who loves them enough to fight for them, their mother, and their family. Listening to what you're saying, I think it's pretty clear you've given up on trying to make it work."

Grandma looks forlorn. I can see her disappointment.

"Did you think that being married would make life easy? Every married couple goes through difficult times. It's normal. It's what happens when two people make a commitment to share the same life. You naturally will not get along all the time. You will argue and you will fight. Welcome to the real world of marriage, Charlie. The question then is what are you going to do about it? Are you going to run away and quit? Which it sounds like you've already made up your mind to do. Or are you going to stand up and work at making your marriage work? You have to decide if you want to be a man of character and integrity. It looks like you may be about to walk down a path where you won't be that kind of man at all."

Grandma is upset.

"Men of character live a life of integrity. When things get tough, they don't run away. You've given Nora and your kids everything they've probably ever wanted. But they don't want the money and all of those things. They may *need* money, but they don't *want* that. What Nora wants, Charlie, is *you*. She wants you to love her. That's it!"

I take another sip of coffee. That's easier than responding.

"You know she's really scared, don't you?"

"No, I don't know that."

"Well, she is. She called yesterday afternoon before I left for dinner."

"She did? Really? Wow! So, what did she have to say?"

"Well, she wanted to know if you were okay. And she is very afraid you're going to walk out on her. She wants to know what happened to the man she married. She admits, too, that she might not be the woman you married. But for Nora, she said it seems you are married more to your law firm than you are to her. Spending so much time at the office. Nights and weekends. Getting home late. Most of the time when you finally get home, she is exhausted. Taking care of the kids, getting them to and from their activities, meals! All of that without much support from you."

"Well, Grandma, what does she expect? I'm working my butt off to pull this deal together and it takes time."

"And she gets that. But she says it gets pretty lonely pulling all of the weight at home by herself. She feels like you are more concerned with making this deal work for a bunch of strangers on the West Coast than you are about living your life in Denver with her and Robbie and Julie."

I don't know what to say.

"For what it's worth, Charlie, I should tell you she was crying. Her voice was soft, almost trembling. The last thing she said was, 'Grandma, don't let him leave me. I won't know what to do without him.'"

If I am honest, I may not know what to do without her either. But we are way past needing each other. I don't understand why everyone doesn't understand that. But I don't think I've ever seen my grandmother this unnerved.

"You know, Charlie, the truth is your grandfather and I were no different."

"Really? I'm not sure I believe that. You two were great whenever we were around."

"Well, everyone is great when other people are around. No one wants anyone else to see what they think is the bad side of their marriage. So, at times we put on a good act, I guess. But we argued. We fought. We disagreed on how to do things. Money was always a big thing. We disagreed at times on the best way to handle your father and his three sisters. It was all part of who we were as a married couple."

She pauses. We both sip our coffee.

"So, when you think about your grandfather, what do you remember most?"

"He was quiet. He didn't seem to have a lot to say. Pretty religious, as I recall. He seemed to know the Bible pretty well. I remember him being gentle. When I helped out on the ranch, he'd have me help bale hay and feed the cattle. Then he'd find time at the end of the day to take me out horseback riding. The way he handled his horse was almost like he was some sort of horse whisperer. He was great.

As we wrapped up the day, I remember how he'd casually slip me a twenty-dollar bill. Those were pretty special times."

"He'd give you twenty dollars?"

"Yeah, twenty bucks. And he would always add, 'Don't tell anyone! Especially Grandma!'"

Grandma is laughing at the memory of her beloved husband. I can see her mind go back to those times in their marriage.

"So, where did Grandpa get all of his books? That's an incredible collection. I can't imagine him having time to read all of them."

"No. He didn't read all of them. He didn't really begin collecting them until after we sold the land. He'd always had this dream to build a little cabin and use it as a getaway to pray and spend some quiet time with God. You're right about him being religious. We never missed Sunday Mass. Sunday for him was a day of rest. He believed in the Commandments and tried his best to live them out. He figured that what he didn't get done by the end of the day on Saturday could always get done on Monday. He was right. He never had any problems on Sunday that couldn't wait and be handled the next day. So, when he wanted to begin collecting books, he wasn't sure how to do that other than go out, spend a lot of money, and buy them. But he heard about some theology professor at Wyoming Catholic College over in Lander, who was retiring and looking to donate his own library to someone who would be interested in taking the books. The college library already had copies of most of them and didn't want them. Ben called the professor, they hit it off, and one weekend we drove over to pick them up. And there we are – what I fondly call the Ben Landis Memorial Catholic Library."

We are both grinning and laughing as we reminisce about this devoted patriarch of the Landis family. Grandma's smile quiets down. I see small tears well up as her eyes become moist with emotion.

"You know, Charlie, I've never told anyone about this. Maybe it's time. Your father never knew. Your aunts never knew. Our friends never knew. But I wonder if there is any reason for me to take this secret to my grave without our family knowing."

I am mesmerized by her discreet demeanor. She is no doubt debating internally whether to divulge some lifetime secret about the man she spent her life with. I hope my eyes are encouraging.

"We met after I moved to Scottsbluff to take a job teaching. Ben was working full time on the ranch, the obvious heir to a fairly successful family enterprise. We fell in love pretty quickly and started talking about marriage and what our life might look like. The night he finally proposed he had tears in his eyes as he held my hand. He said to me, 'Mary, I am asking you tonight to be my wife. I love you so very much and hope I can be the husband you deserve me to be.' Then with tears in his eyes, just like I have in my own right now, he said, 'Mary, I have a secret I have never told anyone. I hope you won't think any less of me. But if we are going to be married, you need to know. I hope and pray tonight that *my* secret can become *our* secret and no one else will ever know.' Of course, I am stunned at what he is saying and wonder what this is and whether I can make a promise like that. But I do love him and I agree that *his* secret is now going to be *our* secret."

I am on the edge of my kitchen chair. Grandma has stopped talking, no doubt weighing the pros and cons of sharing whatever it is for the first time.

"He went on to tell me that because his family needed help on the ranch, he left school in the eighth grade and never finished high school. Because of that and some reading disorder, he never learned how to read or write. His teachers tried to help him, but way back then no one knew how to deal with that other than just keep passing him and letting him move on to the next grade. His parents probably knew, but they were more interested in getting him to help on the ranch than worrying about his grades. He was so embarrassed about it that he never told anyone until he told me the night he proposed."

"But what do you mean he couldn't read or write? What about all of those books?"

"He really hoped after selling the ranch and getting all of the books that he could go back to school and learn to read. But the reading disorder was too much. He said he could never get the letters to quit jumping around. It was really a shame. He wanted it so much, but just couldn't do it."

"So, then when did he learn to read?"

"He never did."

"But what about the leather-bound journal? I saw that in the bookcase."

Grandma's face is serene and peaceful. She is slowing nodding her head, a slight smile on her face, thinking about her compassionate husband and the secret she held in her heart for their entire life.

"But, Grandma, the journal? Do you mean that he was never able to use it?"

"No, he wasn't. Ben had great hopes that one day he would find a way to write something in it. He thought if he could begin to read, then he could finally write down some of his most intimate and personal reflections. He wondered out loud a few times if anyone could read scribbles. We laughed a lot about that."

I am shocked. I know what I read in that journal.

"So, Grandma, you're telling me that the leather-bound journal in the cabin on the bookcase on the right has nothing in it."

"That's right. Nothing. Lots of hopes and dreams on those pages, but no words. He just couldn't do it."

I bolt out of my chair, crash through the kitchen door, and sprint toward the cabin. As I enter the cabin, I slow down trying to gather myself and comprehend what I have just learned about my grandfather.

"This can't be," I whisper to myself.

Edging over to the bookcase, I gently reach out and pull the journal off the shelf. I leaf through the pages. Grandma is right. Not a single word on any of the white pages.

Every page is blank.

# 19

Billy is right where he said he would be. In church, on his knees, praying in the front pew. I'm still processing all that happened with Grandma and the story of Grandpa and his journal. My heart is pounding out of my chest as I slide into the pew next to Billy. As he sits back, his demeanor is characteristically calm. He seems surprised to see me. His voice is a mere whisper.

"Hey, Charlie. I wasn't sure if you'd show up."

"And I didn't expect to be showing up either. Trust me, this was not a planned visit. But I think I need you to help me sort this all out."

"Okay! What's going on?"

As I begin to unfold the series of events from the morning with Grandma, I can tell Billy is perplexed, maybe even a little skeptical. He is listening closely, but I suspect he has to be wondering about the veracity of this story from this wayward and lost friend.

"Wow, Charlie. I'm not sure what to say. And there is no doubt in your mind that you saw the writing and read the words from your grandpa's journal?"

"Absolutely! No doubts at all. It was all there."

Now my mind races back to those intimate moments in the cabin. Perhaps it was some illusion. But no, I read the words. I saw the letters.

"I'm telling you, Billy, it was real. The darkness and the overwhelming fears of our lives, the truth and reality of God, and the consequences of our choices when we are trying to decide whether to quit or not quit! They all took my breath away. I was astonished by the honesty. The intimacy of the words touched the depths of my heart. I couldn't believe what I was reading."

"And your grandfather was unable to read or write, correct?"

"Grandma said that was their one secret absolutely no one else ever knew anything about. Whenever he went to the store, he paid cash. She said he'd just toss down what he figured was more than enough money to pay for everything and wait for the clerk to hand him back the change. When they were first married, Sunday Mass was still said in Latin. So, they would share the same Missal. She said they would sit next to one another, she would open it to the right page and he would glance down now and then to pretend like he was following along and knew what was going on."

"Did your dad know? Or his sisters? Or any other relatives? Did anyone suspect anything?"

"I don't think so. I never remember any of them wondering about that. Grandma did say that she handled all the homework assignments when everyone was in school. That would make sense, since she was a teacher. She said that Grandpa was working so much and so hard that it seemed normal that he would not be involved with any of that. They fooled everyone, I guess."

"I remember from our high school days that your grandpa was pretty religious."

"Yeah, Grandma said she would read to him almost every night from the Bible or some other book on spirituality. She would also help him memorize his favorite scriptures. Radio and television helped him stay current with the news. Apparently he was quite intelligent. He simply couldn't read or write. At least, that's the story."

Billy is still listening. Pulling together his thoughts, no doubt.

"Well, Charlie, here's what I think. It seems to me that the grace of God is pouring into your life in a way that you could have never imagined. I'm thinking it's pretty clear that God doesn't want you to end your marriage. I think he is saying very directly that he needs you to be Nora's husband. He needs you to be that father to Robbie and Julie that you know you want to be. And you can't do any of that if you quit your marriage. Look, Charlie, with all due respect, you know what's right."

"You say that a lot, you know! 'With all due respect!'"

"I know. I get that a lot. I'm only saying it that way because I have a point to make and you should listen up. Pay attention to me and what I'm about to say, because it's important."

"Okay, go ahead."

"So, Charlie, with all due respect, you do know the right thing to do. The world and all of its false promises has yanked you and sucked you into a life you never really wanted. You veered off course when your possessions became more important than the people in your life. Your possessions began to possess you. Now you're so far down the road that you don't know what to do or how to get out of it."

Billy moves a little closer. His whisper is firm and pointed.

"God is in this, Charlie. He is calling you in the depths of your heart to do the right thing. In the Book of the Prophet Jeremiah, it says, 'I will place my law within them, and write it upon their hearts; I will be their God, and they shall be my people.' I think it was St. Bruno who said that 'Almighty God will inscribe in your hearts with

121

his finger not only his love but also the knowledge of his holy law.' I remember an old hymn attributed to St. Ambrose that said, 'Help us, O Lord, to know the truths thy Word imparts are inscribed upon our hearts.' Charlie, you know all of this. No matter what you are thinking or what emotions are flooding your heart about Nora and the mess of your marriage, this is not the time to quit. This is not what you want. I know that and I think you know it, too. If divorcing your sweet Nora was all you wanted to do, you would have gone home two nights ago and ended it. The fact that you drove all the way up here to Scotts-bluff tells me you don't want it all to end. You're just looking for a way out and a way forward."

Billy is right. But I don't know what to do. Coming to grips with my own arrogance and beginning to accept my own greedy drive to be successful at any cost, I can feel the emotions of fear and sorrow begin to well up. The flood of tears starts slowly, but gradually erupts into an avalanche of uncontrollable sobs. Billy reaches over and grabs my heaving shoulders.

"It's okay, Charlie. Just let it go. It's okay. It's okay."

As I try to gather myself, Billy doesn't say anything. He is letting me be myself right now. So raw. So real. He is permitting me to live the moment, giving me a chance to be probably as honest with myself as I have ever been. The sobs settle down. The tears are providing some welcome comfort to my shattered body.

"Let me do the talking, Charlie. Just listen for a minute. God didn't call you to be a lawyer and make lots of money. He called you to a life of love with Nora and your children. He blessed you with the gifts and talents to be a really good lawyer so you could support your family. But God doesn't care how much money you make. He cares about how you use the money to love your wife and children. He doesn't care about what kind of home you live in or what kind of car you drive. God cares about how you love the people he has placed in your life. All of those other things are okay, but those 'things' in our life can get in the way. They can quickly become our gods, those gods with a small 'g.' Life then becomes a great contest to collect 'things' that in the end don't matter. I've been with a lot of people as they have taken their final breath. Not one has ever said to me that they wished they made more money or driven a more expensive car or lived in a bigger house. It doesn't happen, because at that moment, they all know that none of that matters. None of it!"

Billy squeezes my shoulders and I look him in the eye.

"The truth is that life can be very simple, especially when we choose to lead lives based on love. People who decide to live those kinds of unassuming lives don't need their names on companies. They don't need to drive fancy cars or live in big houses. That's all okay, but most of those people don't need or even want those things. They have discovered they can live without what the world tells them they need. Their lives are in some ways hidden. They don't make headlines. They show up every day to see what God might have in mind for the day ahead. It's all about God. Your marriage, Charlie, is your mission in life. Sure you want to be happy, but the real goal is to be holy. Life is fleeting. It's over in an instant. You are only a speck in the great gulf of creation. This life is not our end. There is more. If we believe God is who he says he is, then we have an appointment on the other side of the veil. Your job is to help the people you love, those people God has placed in your life, to know the one, true God and then help them enter the Kingdom he has promised all of us."

"So, where do I go? How can I fix this?"

"First of all, Charlie, you have to know that your love is not a mistake. What you and Nora have is a marriage that was all part of God's plan for the two of you from the beginning. That day in Omaha, when you ran into the back of her little red car, was all part of it. He had to get the two of you together some way. A rainy day, some slick pavement, and a skidding motorcycle all came together in that moment to begin your journey together. All of the ups and the downs, all the good times and the bad times are part of the deal. The question for you now is what are you going to do? Quit? Or get back in the game? Your world and everyone in it are holding their collective breath to see what you are going to do. As I said before, love is all about sacrifice. It's all about being heroic. Jesus gave his life for all of us. You, as a husband and father, are called to give your life for the people you say you love. Now is the time, Charlie."

Billy's soft voice and gentle words have settled me down. An unexpected peace has come over me. Yes, now is the time. I know that. As I bow my head, I find myself saying the words I never thought I could say…or maybe never had the courage to say.

"Bless me, Father, for I have sinned. It's been seven years since my last confession."

# EPILOGUE

### Fr. Bill Donahue

Those two days with Charlie took place near the end of May in the year 1982. Ronald Reagan was President. *E.T., the Extra-Terrestrial* and *Chariots of Fire* were major movie hits, Michael Jackson released his epic *Thriller* album, and the St. Louis Cardinals won the World Series.

Charlie was a changed man after his journey to Scottsbluff. He came to know God in a very deep and compelling way. He had found the proverbial pearl of great price. He would never be the same.

Before he headed home that Saturday night, we talked about the power of forgiveness, especially in a marriage. I told him that I had come to believe the four most important words a husband and wife will ever speak to one another are these – "Will you forgive me?" Apologizing is good. Saying "I'm sorry" is good. But asking for forgiveness requires a "yes" or "no" answer. Sometimes the answer might be "no" or "not yet," but true forgiveness is the foundation of a holy and permanent healing.

I often get the question about forgiving and forgetting. How do I forget what happened? The truth is we don't forget. In real forgiveness what happens is that we will remember the incident or situation, but what goes away is the hurt and the pain. When a married couple can forgive one another and heal the hurts, what gets washed away are the wounds. The pain vanishes like soap suds disappearing down a drain.

I would meet Nora for the first time a few months later. Charlie, Nora, Robbie, and Julie all came to Scottsbluff for a long weekend. We visited with Charlie's grandmother, sat in his grandfather's cabin, and reminisced about everything. We all had a chance to look at his grandpa's journal and marvel again at the grace of God working in the lives of everyone there.

When Nora and I had a moment by ourselves, she shared that she didn't know what to expect when Charlie came back home. He had called on the way, but either didn't want to talk much or emotionally couldn't talk about what happened in Scottsbluff. He got home late and walked into the house with tears in his eyes. He put his arms around her, held her tight, and whispered over and over, "Nora, I am so sorry. I am so sorry. Will you forgive me? Please forgive me."

She said they stayed up until the wee hours of the morning. They talked and they talked. They made love. And they talked some more as the pain and wounds of their marriage were being healed.

Nora told me the man who came home that night was once again the man who slid into her car on a drizzly day in Omaha and then captured her heart. She said it was *that* Charlie she fell in love with and it was *that* man who walked back into their home that Saturday night.

The next day along with Robbie and Julie they went to Mass together as a family. Charlie would later tell me that on that Sunday in church, it felt like he started life over. Everything seemed new. The bloodied, crucified Christ called him as never before to a life of love and sacrifice for Nora, his children, and the people who crossed his path.

I'll tell you this, too. Charlie never forgot the number of years he and Nora were married. He spoke often about their wedding day and its importance. He loved talking about all the memories of that day when they began their life together. He never forgot the date either. June 11, 1966.

By the way, the merger deal with the California firm was completed successfully. That started a new chapter in the lives of everyone involved. But Charlie knew quickly that being a partner in a large, growing legal practice was not a dream anymore. Within a year he negotiated his way out. His partners gave him a lucrative financial package. He and Nora decided to move out of Denver. They sold their home and bought a nice spread on about twenty acres of land a little north of Steamboat Springs in northern Colorado. Charlie then started a small family law practice in Steamboat, where the Landis family became fixtures in the community and in their church, Holy Name Catholic Church. He would say later that he could have made much more money in Denver, but he said God provided and they always had enough.

When Charlie's grandmother passed away, he inherited his grandfather's books. He built a large wooden bookcase for the entire library. It filled parts of two walls in his small den. The leather-bound journal became a prized possession he placed next to the Bible he prayed with every morning.

Charlie and I remained good friends in the ensuing years. He even convinced me I should buy a motorcycle. Which I did! A few times a year Charlie and Nora would meet me somewhere around Estes Park and the Rocky Mountain National Forest. We would then bike around northern Colorado or southern Wyoming for a few days. We had a great time biking through some of God's most wondrous creations. The mountains with the herds of elk and moose, the big horn sheep, the chipmunks, and those friendly yellow-bellied marmots were spectacular.

I would describe Charlie and Nora's marriage as a very good one. Not perfect, for sure, but they recognized the importance of their relationship to one another and their children. Yes, they disagreed at times. Yes, they fought at times. But they learned how to understand their differences, heal the hurts, and forgive one another.

Charlie had a stubborn streak in him. For some reason, he wanted to be or thought he needed to be right all the time. That was not one of his most endearing qualities.

Charlie and Nora also decided to see if God might bless them with more children. Robbie and Julie would become a big brother and sister to Ben, Mary, Teresa, and Catherine. Ben and Mary were twins born around Nora's fortieth birthday. Still praying about having more children, Charlie and Nora later adopted Teresa and Catherine.

Their life wasn't without tragedy and heartache. Little Teri was diagnosed with a rare form of childhood leukemia. She battled like a trooper but lost the fight. Teri was four years old when she died.

Shortly after they celebrated their 40th wedding anniversary Nora began showing signs of what turned out to be Alzheimer's disease. She would routinely misplace her car keys. She wasn't able to remember the names of good friends. By the time they celebrated their 50th wedding anniversary, Nora was a shell of the lady she once was. But Charlie loved her through everything. When she became angry and frustrated with the way her life was deteriorating, Charlie would comfort her in any way he could. He would hold her hand, put his arm around her, or simply whisper words of love and encouragement.

I remember one moment in their home as everyone gathered to celebrate their fifty years of marriage. Their children, and now their nine grandchildren, along with dozens of friends were all there. I was sitting quietly with Charlie and Nora in one corner of their family room. Charlie was reminiscing about their marriage. He talked about how they met and fell in love. He nostalgically remembered so many of the good times, the bad times, and how grateful he was for the life God had blessed them with.

Nora was sitting there with what had become a customary blank look on her face. Suddenly she seemed to almost come back to life. She slowly reached over and grabbed Charlie's hand. She raised her head and looked directly at him. Her eyes seemed amazingly alive. Her voice was only a whisper.

"Thank you, Charlie. I love you so very much."

With those words, Nora looked away. The blank stare returned. I have no doubt it was a moment of unimaginable grace. God had given a nine-word gift to Charlie that he would never forget.

Nora would live another year and a few months before the disease would take her life. Charlie was so thankful for the life they lived together. In fact, he never forgot the number of days he and Nora were permitted to share with one another. From that June wedding day to the day Nora died, the total number of days was 18,718. They lived a blessed life and Charlie knew that.

And Charlie?

Well, Charlie died last week.

His funeral is today.

# THE FAREWELL

## The Funeral Mass for Charles Patrick Landis

Good morning. I am Fr. Bill Donahue. It has been a great gift for me to be here and concelebrate this Mass to celebrate the life of my friend, Charlie. Thanks to the family for permitting me to say a few words before we say farewell and depart. As many of you may know, we were good friends growing up in Scottsbluff, Nebraska. We were both altar boys in one of our local Catholic churches. We played baseball together. We hung out together. For almost two decades after high school we lost touch as we each went our separate ways.

But through what I believe was the hand of God, our paths would cross again in May of 1982. I will spare you the details. Suffice it to say our reunion was tumultuous. Through the anger, the frustration, and the peace Charlie eventually found, the two of us became very good friends. Along with his precious wife, Nora, and their six children, all of us through the years have maintained a strong, long-distance friendship.

I think I can say that at one point in Charlie's life, the world was having its way with him. He was into success and power and prestige. His ego was as big as the state of Alaska. He sometimes described himself as a jerk. By the way, I can attest to that. From what I hear, a lot of people would have agreed. His relentless pride was driving him to be the best lawyer he could be. Back then it was all about making money and accumulating as many "things" as he could. He believed his worth would be measured by the size of his home, or the kind of car he drove, or having his name on the letterhead of a large law firm.

But that all changed when he had an unforgettable encounter with God during the two days we spent together in 1982. He came to realize that God wasn't calling him to be the best lawyer he could be, but to be the best husband and father he could be. He knew for that to happen, things in his life would have to change. And, as I think you know, he changed them.

When Charlie began to trust completely in Christ, his life was transformed. Life then for Charlie, Nora, and their children would never be the same. He came to this community to live what he often described as "a hidden life." He didn't live his life in the big wide world we all think of, but rather in this small world here in this community. I know his hope was that all of you would not remember him so much as a friend or as the lawyer who helped you when you needed some legal advice, but as the man who loved his wife and children and grandchildren the best he could. He wanted to be a family man first and a good lawyer second.

Charlie often talked with me about his favorite Gospel. It's found in the 15th Chapter of the Gospel of John. The Vine and the Branches! That Scripture says that Jesus is the Vine and we are the branches. Charlie came to realize that his life needed to be rooted in Jesus Christ alone. Charlie knew that he was only a mere branch on the vine. He didn't have to be the biggest branch or the strongest branch. He only needed to be the branch that God was calling him to be.

When Charlie was diagnosed with his pancreatic cancer, he knew the days in front of him were going to be short. About a month ago, when he and the doctors came to grips with the reality that the cancer treatments were not working, Charlie called me. We talked for a long time. We both shed a tear or two. He asked me, if I could, to be here and concelebrate this Mass. He also asked if I would share a letter he wrote to all of you. He asked me, too, to promise that I wouldn't open it until now.

So, here goes! These words are from your father, your grandfather, your good friend, and my very good companion, Charlie.

*T*hanks for being here, Everyone. Nothing better to do today, huh? In case you might have forgotten, I'm the one in the wooden casket in the center aisle up near the front.

*(Billy, this is where you point to the casket!!)*

*I will say that this life now behind me was an incredible adventure. I hope everyone knows that I really loved my wife. Nora was truly the best thing that ever happened to me.*

*And you children and you grandchildren, what incredible blessings you have been to both of us. Life was full and fun and rich, all because of you. You drove us a little crazy now and then, but we truly thank the Good God for permitting us to be your parents and grandparents.*

*And to all of you, our good friends, I can't thank you enough for the way you walked with us on this journey, for the ways you loved us, and so often dared us to be the best husband and wife we could be. For the times you knew we needed to heal some hurt in our marriage and challenged us to seek forgiveness, thank you for your love and compassion in what were often dark times for the two of us.*

*Our faith tells us that this life we live here is fleeting. I think right now I might be able to attest to that. (Smiley face goes here!) Our faith also tells us that there is a life beyond this life. I resolutely believe that. I also believe that right now I might very well be meeting face to face with the God of All Creation. One more thing our faith tells us is that once we enter Heaven, we can pray and intercede for all of those we have left behind. So, you can trust me that I am doing that right now for each one of you.*

*One of my prayers will be that you understand the truth of our humanity. Pontius Pilate asked the question of Jesus before his crucifixion: "What is truth?" That is probably a question all of us ask at some time in one way or another. Ultimately it will be a question we will all have to answer some day.*

*The reality, I have discovered, is that spirituality is the very core of our being. There is a famous quote that puts a lot of life into context for me.*

*"We have to remember that we are not human beings having spiritual experiences. Rather we are spiritual beings having human experiences."*

*So, when life for you becomes difficult, when you are faced with the steep paths of your own journey, when you don't know what to do with your fears, your insecurity, your loneliness, the dark parts of your own life, please remember that someone is praying for you. I will be asking the God who created all of us to be with you, to bless you, to be generous and charitable, to touch your life with love, hope, and the Peace of Jesus Christ this day and every day in front of you.*

*My hope, too, is that when life feels good and things are going your way (as they often will) that you will pause for a moment to recognize that the hand of God has gifted you with yet another one of life's many blessings. (God, by the way, has a habit of doing that.) He is a good and gracious God who has great plans for all of your lives. My prayer is that you will believe that, trust in Him always, and follow Him wherever He chooses to lead you.*

*Scripture tells us that the road is narrow that leads to life. For me, choosing the narrow gate has made all the difference. May all of you choose to enter through the narrow gate. It took me some time to find that. My hope is that you might find it sooner than I did.*

*The greatest blessing in my life has been to be a husband, father, grandfather, and friend to all of you. Until we meet again, God bless you and thank you for touching my life with your incredible love and compassion. I am forever grateful.*

Charlie was buried next to Nora in their family plot. Little Teri is buried there, too. Their headstones are reminders of the life they lived together and how God called them to live it as a sign of extraordinary love and fidelity, a living witness to the love of God. For Charlie and Nora, through all of the ups and the downs, the good times and the tough times, their marriage covenant to love and honor one another all the days of their lives provided the foundation for the five decades of their marriage.

It was all part of the deal.

# ABOUT THE AUTHOR

Chuck Neff is a veteran broadcast journalist. Most recently he has worked as a Show Host of *The Inner Life*™ on Relevant Radio,® a national Catholic radio network airing in more than 170 markets. A graduate of the University of Missouri School of Journalism, he has worked in radio and television as a news reporter in Chicago, Denver, St. Louis, and Terre Haute, Indiana. Chuck has also traveled the world producing documentaries in the Holy Land, as well as South America and Eastern Europe.

Over his career Chuck and his production company have been awarded 15 regional Emmys. He has also received dozens of other national and regional awards for outstanding programming. In 1999, he coordinated the worldwide television pool coverage for the Pastoral Visit of Saint John Paul II to the Archdiocese of Saint Louis.

Chuck and his wife, Judy, were a presenting team couple for Worldwide Marriage Encounter for nine years. In the Archdiocese of Saint Louis they helped start Retrouvaille, a weekend for hurting marriages. They live in Chesterfield, Missouri. They have four children and nine grandchildren.

# ACKNOWLEDGMENTS

While the locations and history depicted in this story are based on actual events and locations, the characters are fictional. Some of the anecdotes are based on actual events in the life of the author. Thanks to the friends and acquaintances who provided those special, real, and honest moments. If you recognize a story you could have been part of, it likely is you. I extend a heartfelt thank you.

Special thanks to:

Fr. John Burns, Fr. Albert Haase, OFM, Fr. Rick Heilman, Fr. Sam Martin, Fr. Burke Masters, Fr. Douglas McKay, Fr. Kevin Schroeder, and Fr. Richard Simon for their stories and insights

Jerald H Lucas – Historic Storyteller, Scottsbluff, Nebraska

Barb Netherland – Library of the Plains Museum, Scottsbluff, Nebraska

Terri Calvert – Director of Religious Education, St. Agnes Catholic Church, Scottsbluff, Nebraska

Angie Fisher – Director of Communications, Diocese of Grand Island, Nebraska

Lee Rodriquez – Director of the Army ROTC at Washington University, Saint Louis, Missouri

Leslie Lynch, Cathy Gilmore, Sally Guignon, Rosie Havey, Ruth Kaufman and Theresa Karutz – the manuscript editors who provided their masterful touches to ensure the need for clarity and brevity. Their attention to detail eliminated all of the annoying typos.

Dave Martin – my good friend who inspired me to keep writing with the simple question – "How's the book coming?"

Rick Myers, *Chasing Light Photography*, for his extraordinary talent and permission to use the images of Scotts Bluff on the cover of *The Deal*.

And Zip Rzeppa and *Mater Media* for taking a chance on a first-time author.

Scottsbluff, Nebraska, is the hometown of Chuck Neff's father, Chuck, Sr. In 1898 Henry Warren Neff, Chuck's grandfather, is said to have gotten off a train where the railroad tracks ended. That would have been Scottsbluff. He started a lumber company and was one of the first mayors in the community. A heartfelt thank you to everyone who helped in pulling together the research on this project. Your cordial hospitality was amazing and most appreciated.

*Carr & Neff Lumber Company*

*Scotts Bluff National Monument*